Helfried Kodré
Vedere l'invisibile

Autoren / Authors
Ellen Maurer Zilioli

Wolfgang Prohaska
Karl Bollmann

Arnoldsche
Art Publishers

Impressum / Imprint

Helfried Kodré

© 2006 ARNOLDSCHE Art Publishers, Stuttgart
und die Autoren/and the authors

Alle Rechte vorbehalten. Vervielfältigung und Wiedergabe auf jegliche Weise (grafisch, elektronisch und fotomechanisch sowie der Gebrauch von Systemen zur Datenrückgewinnung) – auch in Auszügen – nur mit schriftlicher Genehmigung der ARNOLDSCHEN Verlagsanstalt GmbH, Liststraße 9, D–70180 Stuttgart. / All rights reserved. No part of this work may be reproduced or used in any forms or by any means (graphic, electronic or mechanical, including photocopying or information storage and retrieval systems) without written permission from the copyright holders.

Autoren / Authors
Ellen Maurer Zilioli
Wolfgang Prohaska
Karl Bollmann

Buchgestaltung und Layout / Book Design and Layout
Frank Philippin, Billy Kiossoglou
Brighten the Corners, Stuttgart & London

Offset-Reproduktionen / Offset-Reproductions
Repromayer, Reutlingen

Druck / Printing
Leibfarth & Schwarz, Dettingen/Erms

Dieses Buch wurde gedruckt auf 100% chlorfrei gebleichtem Papier (entspricht damit dem TCF-Standard). /
This book has been printed on paper that is 100% free of chlorine bleach in conformity with TCF standards.

Bibliographic information published by Die Deutsche Bibliothek: Die Deutsche Bibliothek lists this publication in the Deutsche Nationalbibliografie; detailed bibliographic data is available on the Internet at http://dnb.ddb.de.

ISBN 3-89790-239-7
ISBN 13: 9783897902398

Made in Europe, 2006

Bildnachweis / Photo credits
Alle Abbildungen von/All illustrations by Helfried Kodré, Wien, außer/with exception of: Petra Zimmermann, Wien (Abb./ill. S./p. 31)

Titelabbildung / Cover illustration
Brosche/Brooch, 2006, s. Abb./ill. 81

Die Publikation wurde gefördert durch / Published with generous support from:

BUNDESKANZLERAMT ▪ KUNST

Bundeskanzleramt Österreich, Wien
Schmuckmuseum Pforzheim
Galerie Slavik, Wien

Inhalt / Contents

Helfried Kodré

6
Ellen Maurer Zilioli
Helfried Kodré – Geordnete Gestaltung
Helfried Kodré – Structural Design

14
Wolfgang Prohaska
Zu Helfried Kodrés künstlerischer Physiognomie
An Artistic Profile of Helfried Kodré

22
Karl Bollmann
Warum Schmuck?
Why Jewellery?

33
Arbeiten von Helfried Kodré 1990–2006
The Work of Helfried Kodré 1990–2006

91
Anhang
Appendix

5	Textbeiträge	Essays
	Ellen Maurer Zilioli, Wolfgang Prohaska und Karl Bollmann	Ellen Maurer Zilioli, Wolfgang Prohaska and Karl Bollmann

Ellen Maurer Zilioli
Helfried Kodré – Structural Design

"Geometry is what exists permanently." (Plato)

A profoundly Constructive concept undoubtedly underlies Helfried Kodré's work, what is more, a world-view in which the square and the cube play a leading role. They form the basis and starting-point of numerous Kodré compositions. The pieces he produced as far back as 1970 already reveal indications of this even though the structures articulating those works are counteracted and modulated by the fluid, soft contours of the organic aesthetic he cultivated then, supplemented by motifs that seem floral and vegetal. During his studio collaboration with Elisabeth Defner (1962–1975), Kodré tended to be viewed as a follower of Eugen Mayer, head of the jewellery class at the Akademie für angewandte Kunst in Vienna (Academy of Applied Arts; now a university) and, moreover – indeed almost inevitably – in connection with an updated version of the interpretation of jewellery that had been created by the early 20th-century reform movements.[1] Consequently, Defner and Kodré were celebrated, so to speak, as the "best successors to the Viennese Secession"[2] – a conditional classification that was only justified from the standpoint of the time, with which Kodré, incidentally, does not identify.

Defner, as a pupil of Mayer's, brought a naturalistic approach as her contribution to this relationship and artistic collaboration, one from which Kodré differed and increasingly moved away from in so far as he espoused ordering principles that tended towards abstraction and had his own distinctive way of composing individual constituents and mounting them. The romanticising, quasi lyrical adaption of natural motifs was certainly pervasive then; after all, they asserted themselves in poetry and music as well after 1945 with a certain degree of consistency and perhaps this variant of existentially working through wartime and post-war reality merged to an even greater

[1] Cf on this Antonia Kühnel (ed.), *Re-view. Aspekte Österreichischer Schmuckkunst*, exhib. cat., Vienna 2003.

[2] Karl Schollmayer, *Neuer Schmuck – ornamentum humanum*, Tübingen 1974, p. 154.

Brosche/Brooch, 1969/70   Brosche/Brooch, 1971

Brosche/Brooch, 1971

trische Disziplinierung von Natursymbolik bereits in der Wiener Werkstätte vorgeprägt waren und dass die Lehre Eugen Mayers Überlegungen zum Raum-Masse-Verhältnis, also einer „raumgliedernden" Ästhetik, berücksichtigte. Er sprach von „Durchbrechung der Fläche", von „einfachen planimetrischen Figuren", von „Form als gesetzmäßiger Spannung im Raum" und so weiter.[3] Prinzipiell verbindet ihn das mit Kodrés Schmuckgestaltung, auch wenn diese in der Anwendung ein völlig anderes Gesicht erhält. Gleichzeitig spiegeln die Aussagen Mayers, wenn man sich vor allem im Gegensatz dazu seine Arbeiten vor Augen führt, den generellen Diskurs um Abstraktion und Realismus in der Kunst der 1950er Jahre wieder, aus dem die folgende Generation dann ihre Konsequenzen zog.

Kodré hat diesen Fond aufgesogen, aber auch weiterverarbeitet, im Sinne einer Reduktion, eines Herausfilterns von immanenten Qualitäten. 1975 etwa liefert ein Armreif den Hinweis auf einige Aspekte, welche in Zukunft stilbildenden Charakter gewinnen sollten – vor dem Hintergrund von Minimalismus, Pop und Konzept Art (siehe Abb. unten rechts).[4] Ein für die Ära typisches Stück und doch weit über die virulenten Tendenzen hinausweisend. Den Akzent setzen Kreis und Viereck, durch vertikale Lamellen segmentiert und facettiert. Gold und Silber paaren sich mit Stahl. Den Ton geben, wie stets bei Kodré, die bewährten Metalle der Goldschmiedetradition an, während der Stahl den zeitgenössischen technischen Bezug zur Moderne signalisiert. An einem solchen Ausgleich zwischen Gegenwart und klassischem Schmuckdenken wird sich Helfried Kodré letztlich auch weiterhin orientieren.

Kurz darauf hat Helfried Kodré das Schmuckmachen unterbrochen (1976–1991) und wandte sich seinem ursprünglichen Interesse zu. Er studierte Kunstgeschichte, promovierte und lehrte schließlich an der Universität Wien.

[3] Vgl. Verena Formanek, *Wiener Schmuck. Tendenzen 1936–1991*, Wien 1992, S. 11f.

[4] Vgl. Abbildung in *Re-view*, a.a.O., S. 33, Nr. 29.

extent with artistic strivings in Vienna and Austria as a whole.

Of course it cannot be denied that stylisation and the geometric disciplining of natural symbolism had been prefigured in the Wiener Werkstätte and that Eugen Mayer's teaching took into consideration thoughts on the relationship between space and mass, that is, an aesthetic that "articulated space". Mayer spoke of "breaking through the surface", of "simple, planimetric figurations", of "form as regulated tension in space" and so on.[3] In principle, all that links him with Kodré's approach to designing jewellery even though in practice Kodré makes it look entirely different. At the same time, Mayer's pronouncements, especially if one looks at his work, reflect the general discourse on abstraction and realism in 1950s art, from which the generation that followed would draw its own conclusions.

Kodré absorbed this foundation but also developed it further in the sense that he reduced it, filtering its immanent qualities from it. A 1975 bangle, for instance, provides a clue to some aspects which would in future assume style-generating character – against the background of Minimalism, Pop and Concept art (see ill. down right).[4] A piece typical of that era, yet pointing far ahead of the trends rampant at the time. The keynote was set by circle and square, segmented by vertical lamellae and faceted. Gold and silver were coupled with steel. As always in Kodré's work, the tried and tested materials of the goldsmithing tradition were paramount whereas steel signalised a contemporary technical reference to Modernism. Helfried Kodré would ultimately continue to lean towards equilibrating the present and the classical conception of jewellery in this way.

Not long afterwards Helfried Kodré stopped making jewellery for a while (1976–1991) and returned to what had

[3] Cf Verena Formanek, *Wiener Schmuck. Tendenzen 1936–1991*, Vienna 1992, pp. 11f.

[4] See the illustration in *Re-view*, loc. cit., pp. 33, no. 29.

Armband/Bracelet, 1971, Schmuckmuseum Pforzheim

Armband/Bracelet, 1975

Eine radikale Entscheidung, vor allem auch angesichts unmittelbar einsetzender, früher Erfolge: 1967 der Bayerische Staatspreis, 1968 die Teilnahme am legendären Ersten Internationalen Symposium für Silberschmuck in Jablonec/CSSR, zum Beispiel, und beides für einen Autodidakten sicherlich nicht von geringer Bedeutung. Es gab allerdings einen schwerwiegenden Anlass für den Abschied: eine zunehmende „Verkünstelung" des Schmucks, das heißt den Zwang des Schmucks hin zur Kunst und vor allem dessen Dogmatisierung und Ideologisierung, unter Umständen auf Kosten der Schmuckidentität. Mit diesen Entwicklungen konnte sich Kodré nicht anfreunden. Nach Jahren zog er sein persönliches Resümee in einem veröffentlichten Text.[5]

Er beobachtete also die experimentelle Radikalisierung und Grenzüberschreitung seines Genres auf internationaler Ebene mit Abstand, um schließlich – trotzdem und von einem neuen, autonomen Standort ausgehend – 1992 wieder als Goldschmied tätig zu werden. Seitdem gibt es zwei Werkphasen, die man geneigt ist, in Beziehung zu setzen, was aber doch nicht immer so recht gelingt, weil die erste sich nicht so klar herauskristallisieren will und die zweite dagegen eine definitiv unabhängige Position formuliert. Sicher, der Autor ist derselbe, er hat Erfahrungen durchlebt und seine Schlüsse gezogen, und daher präsentiert sich der aktuelle Werkabschnitt als gereifte, geläuterte, als konsequent durchdachte Ästhetik.

Wenn wir diesen Weg Kodrés nun rekonstruieren wollen, so begegnen uns zunächst Objekte von betont skulpturaler Qualität. Ohrschmuck, der an Gesimsfragmente antiker oder antikisierender Renaissance-Bauwerke erinnert. Broschen erscheinen als schmale Stege und Stabbündel, gespalten, geknickt, gestuft und getreppt – in Silber, seltener akzentuiert durch Goldgelenke, die Oberflächen oft leicht schraffiert, punziert, auf jeden Fall mattiert und damit zurückgenommen

[5] Helfried Kodré, „Nouvelle Cuisine – oder zurück an den Anfang. Die Schmuckkunst-Szene der 1970er Jahre", in: *ebd.*, S. 68–71.

originally interested him. He studied art history, took his doctorate and then taught at Vienna University. A radical decision, especially when one considers the early success that set in immediately: being awarded the Bavarian State Prize in 1967 and participating in the legendary 1968 International Symposium for Silver Jewellery in Jablonec, CSSR, just to mention two examples, both of which certainly must have meant quite a bit to an entirely self-taught artist. There was, however, a weighty reason for his departure: the growing "artiness" of jewellery, that means, the compulsion towards art in jewellery and especially the freighting of this trend with dogma and ideology, under some circumstances at the expense of the identity of jewellery *qua* jewellery. Kodré had little or no use for this development. Years later he would settle his personal accounts with it in a published text.[5]

He observed the experimental radicalisation and boundary infringements of his chosen genre occurring on an international level with detachment, only to again resume work as a goldsmith in 1992 – despite all this and starting from a new, autonomous position. Since then there have been two phases of his work which one is tempted to relate to one another but this linkage is not always so convincing because the first stage cannot really be clearly defined while the second, on the other hand, formulates a definitively independent stance. Certainly, the auteur of both is one and the same; he has lived through experiences and drawn his conclusions from them. Consequently, the current phase of his work is revealed as a mature, transfigured and consistently thought-out aesthetic.

If we want to reconstruct the route Kodré has taken, we first encounter objects of emphatically sculptural quality. Ear jewellery reminiscent of fragments of cornices from ancient architecture or Renaissance buildings in the ancient

[5] Helfried Kodré, "Nouvelle Cuisine – oder zurück an den Anfang. Die Schmuckkunst-Szene der 1970er Jahre", in: *ibid.*, pp. 68–71.

Brosche/Brooch, 1971

Brosche/Brooch, 1971

Brosche/Brooch, 1971

Anhänger/Pendant, 1974/75

in ihrer stofflichen Präsenz. Winkel- und Schalenelemente, Türmchen und Sockel, kleine Zylinder- und Quaderblöcke, in ein enges, symbiotisches Verhältnis zueinander gesetzt, miteinander verschmelzend, ineinander verschachtelt, auseinander hervorwachsend, eine eindeutige Referenz an die Passion des Kunsthistorikers Kodré für moderne Skulptur und Architektur als eine Quelle seiner Inspiration. Doch geht es nie wirklich um konkrete Vorbilder, sondern um ein gemeinsames Bedürfnis nach objektivierten Formen, durchdrungen von einem stilistischen Bekenntnis.

Ringe – ein besonderes Kapitel im Schmuckschaffen Kodrés, der die Kombination aus Kreis, der um den Finger gesteckt wird, und bekrönendem, montiertem und attributivem Aufsatz verweigert und den Ring vielmehr als einen geschlossenen Körper wahrnimmt und konzipiert. Und so sehen sie auch aus: kleine kompakte, geometrische Einheiten, deren stiftartige Ausläufer die farblich exakt ausgewählten Steine enthalten – aus einem Guss quasi und weniger der Zierde, dem Dekor huldigend, als vielmehr der konstruktiven Identität.

Ein weiteres Thema: quadratische Gold-, Silber- und Stahlflächen, mehrfach geschichtet, leicht aus der Mitte verschoben und gedreht – Broschen als Relief. Die räumliche Wirkung wird unterstrichen und forciert durch Faltungen der einzelnen Ebenen – als eingeknickte Ecken, umgeschlagene Kanten, nach vorne geklappte Teile zuunterst liegender Elemente. Dadurch werden alle Materialien auch sichtbar: Stahl glänzt, Silber dagegen wird geschwärzt, Gold bleibt Gold. Den bildhaften Faktor bringen die mit grafischen, gestrichelten, punktierten oder kräftig schraffierten Mustern überdeckten Felder ein, eine besondere Finesse dabei das von Goldpunkten in regelmäßigen Linien durchzogene Silberkarree. Manchmal enthält das äußere Quadrat ein Inneres und erweitert auf diese Weise die strukturelle Komplexität. Von der Fläche in den Raum expandieren weitere Arbeiten,

manner. Brooches emerge as narrow fillets and bundles of rods, bent, tiered and stepped – in silver, only rarely set off with gold joints, the surfaces often lightly hatched, punced, in any case matt and, therefore, with their physical substance visually downgraded. Angular and bowl-like elements, little towers and plinths, small cylinders and ashlar blocks, placed in a close symbiotic interrelationship, fused into one another, nested, growing out of and apart from one another, an unequivocal reference to Kodré's passion as an art historian for modern sculpture and architecture as a source of inspiration. Yet there is never really any question of concrete models but rather a concomitant need for objectivised forms informed by a commitment to style.

Rings – a special chapter in Kodré's work; rejecting the combination of a circle put on a finger and crowned by a bezel and attributive mount, he instead perceives and conceives the ring as a complete, autonomous entity. And that is what his rings look like: small compact geometric units, whose pin-like outliers have been given stones chosen precisely for their colour – a perfect whole, as it were, that pays tribute less to adornment, to the decorative than to Constructive identity.

Another theme: square surfaces of gold, silver and steel, multi-layered, shifted slightly off-centre and turned – brooches as relief. The spatial effect is underscored and re-enforced by the individual levels being folded – as inverted corners, everted edges, folded out parts of elements lying at the bottom. Thus the properties of all materials are rendered visible: steel gleams, although silver is blackened, but gold remains gold. The pictorial factor is introduced by fields covered in graphic, streaked, dotted or forcefully hatched patterns; particularly sophisticated is a silver square shot through like tartan with gold dots in regular lines.

vorwiegend Broschen, die ebenfalls um das zentrale Motiv des Quadrates kreisen, das Thema allerdings als plastisches Gebilde, als Volumen definieren und aufbauen. Hier verbünden sich zwei- und dreidimensionales Bestreben auf eindringlichste Weise. Rundrohre oder schmale Schienen aus geschwärztem Silber umschließen einen Innenhof, dessen Seiten gegeneinander versetzt und sich an den Enden überschneidend verlaufen. Die Fassungen überlagern einander also mit einer leichten Verschiebung. Das verschafft Dichte, so bildet sich körperliche Substanz heraus.

Dynamisch und emotional, ja geradezu mit einer dekonstruktivistischen Note versehen, artikuliert sich das Kräftespiel in jenen Schmuckstücken, die sich aus verschlungenen und miteinander verzahnten Rechtecken und Quadraten zusammensetzen – ein immer wieder erstaunlich ausgetüfteltes System, das genauestes Studium und exakte technische Vorgehensweise erzwingt, denn alles wird bis ins Kleinste kalkuliert, geschnitten, montiert und gelötet. Die Komposition bleibt stets einsichtig und nachvollziehbar. Kodré vermeidet jegliche Verunklärung. Trotzdem ruft die Vervielfältigung der Module einen verwirrenden und irritierenden Eindruck hervor. Eine große Arbeit kann etwa bis zu drei Quadrate und vier Rechtecke umfassen.

Neuere Werke dieser Art weisen kleine eingelassene Farbfelder, Lapislazuli, Glas, Türkis, an den Ausläufern auf. Kodré hat sich mit dem Kolorit stets sehr zurückgehalten. Umso eindringlicher und signalhafter schießen diese Akzente aus den Kompositionen hervor.

Bildhauerische Arbeiten bilden das zweite Standbein des Künstlers. Was sich im Schmuck oft eher andeutet – wie etwa die Referenz auf das Motiv des Kubus – erfährt in der Skulptur eine Intensivierung. Hier tritt die Grundform in vollem Umfang in Erscheinung, hier dreht sich der künstlerische Diskurs um die Konstruktion von Gehäusen,

Sometimes an outer square is given an inner one and in this way its structural complexity is enhanced.

Other works, primarily brooches, expand from the surface into space. They also revolve around the central motif of the square, albeit defining and building up the theme as sculptural configurations, as volume. Here strivings for two and three dimensions are powerfully united. Round tubing or narrow fillets of blackened silver enclose an inner court, whose sides are out of alignment so that their ends overlap. As a result, the settings overlap with a slight displacement. This creates density; thus is physical substance formed.

Dynamically and emotionally, indeed tinged with a Deconstructivist bias, the play of forces is articulated in those pieces of jewellery which are composed of interleaved and interlocked rectangles and squares – a sophisticated system that never ceases to astonish, exacting as it does precise study and accurate application of technique since everything to be cut, mounted and soldered is calculated down to the last detail. The composition always remains clear and intelligible. Kodré eschews mystification in every way. Still the multiplication of modules creates a bewildering and disturbing impression. A work on a large scale can, for instance, comprise up to three squares and four rectangles.

More recent works of this kind boast small inset colour fields – lapis lazuli, glass, turquoise – on the extensions. Kodré has always been an extremely reticent colourist. All the more urgently, therefore, do these touches of colour shoot out like signals from such compositions.

Sculptural works are the second pillar of the artist's work. What is often merely suggested in his jewellery – the reference to the cube motif, for instance – is intensified in his sculpture. Here the basic form is entirely overt; here the

von Innen- und Außensphäre, um Aufspaltung und Skelettierung von Volumen und dessen Vermessung im Raum, um die Auslotung von Spannung und Dynamik. Es handelt sich quasi um ein dreidimensionales Koordinatensystem, im Kern der Würfelkörper, der keine kompakte Masse darstellt, sondern eine lediglich gedachte Dimension, von Maßstäben und Verstrebungen regelrecht erfüllt und durchwandert. Die mathematisch exakte Figur gerät mit der Zeit in Bewegung, neigt sich zur Seite, streckt und dehnt die Komposition in verschiedene Richtungen. Die ursprüngliche Ordnung scheint aus der Mitte zu streben und ihre Begrenztheit sprengen zu wollen.

Wenn man sich die Geschichte der Goldschmiedekunst vor Augen führt, war die streng konstruktive Abstraktion als ästhetische Strategie eigentlich nie ein dauerhaftes und zentrales Anliegen. Sie entstammt eher dem Kanon der traditionellen Kunstgattungen und der historischen Moderne.

Als Kodré 1992 zum Schmuck zurückkehrte, war vieles geschehen. Es hatten sich verschiedene Strömungen entwickelt, die den Bruch mit der Konvention forderten, bis hin zu Provokation, Performance und totaler Grenzüberschreitung. Allerdings hat sich vor allem im österreichischen Schmuck ein Bewusstsein für die handwerkliche Ausführung und gleichzeitig für eine geometrische Formgebung stets erhalten. Helfried Kodré bezieht vor diesem Hintergrund in gewisser Weise eine „klassisch" zu nennende Position. Er fühlt sich weiterhin dem Schmuck als Schmuck verpflichtet, auch wenn seine Gestaltungsmittel eine lange Kunst-Geschichte aufweisen und seine Arbeiten dadurch mit dieser vernetzen.

Wir wissen: Kubus und Quadrat sind seit alters Symbole von idealen Maßverhältnissen. Darin spiegelt sich die Vorstellung von Kosmos, von Dauerhaftigkeit und Perfektion, von Regelmäßigkeit und Göttlichkeit. Zum

artistic discourse revolves around the construction of casings, of inner and outer spheres, focuses on splitting up and skeletonising volume and measuring it in space, on plumbing the properties of tension and dynamics. What is at stake here is a three-dimensional system of co-ordinates, so to speak, at the core of the cube, which does not represent compact mass but rather entirely fills out and pervades a purely imaginary dimension. With time, the mathematically exact figure starts to move, tilts to the side, extending and expanding the composition in different directions. The original arrangement seems to be striving to leave the centre as if struggling to transgress its limitations.

When one looks back on the history of goldsmithing, stringently Constructive abstraction as an aesthetic strategy was never a lasting and pivotal concern. On the contrary, it comes from the canon of the traditional art genres and historical Modernism.

By the time Kodré returned to jewellery in 1992, much had happened. Various trends had developed which ranged from a call for breaking with convention to provocation, Performance and total infringement of boundaries. However, in Austrian jewellery especially, a conscious appreciation of craftsmanship accompanied by geometric design has never been lost. Viewed against this background, Helfried Kodré takes up a stance that might in a certain sense be termed "classical". He continues to feel committed to jewellery *qua* jewellery even though the means he uses to design it go far back in art history and, therefore, enmesh his works with it.

As we know: the cube and the square have been the symbols of ideal proportion from time immemorial. In them is reflected the idea of cosmos, of permanence and perfection, of regularity and divinity. The Heavenly Jerusalem of the Apocalypse, for instance, is described as a

 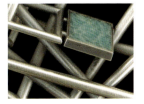

Beispiel wird das himmlische Jerusalem der Apokalypse als Kubus beschrieben.⁶ In der gesamten Philosophie repräsentieren die geometrischen Grundformen die vollkommene Verschmelzung von Materie und Geist, die Durchdringung von Raum und Zeit, für Kant eine Gegebenheit *a priori*. Seit Heraklit, Aristoteles und Platon manifestiert sich darin der Prozess von Abstraktion als Ergebnis von Erkenntnis und Erfahrung humaner Seinsbedingungen. In der Kunst findet sie ihren Ausdruck als gegenstandsloses Bild oder ornamentales Zeichen. Wir kennen Dürers *Melancolia*, wir kennen Proportionslehren und Bemühungen um objektive Größenverhältnisse und mathematische Korrektheit planimetrischer Zeichenschemata seit der Antike. Quadrat und Kubus fungieren dabei als die wesentlichen Werkzeuge.

Die Abstraktion des 20. Jahrhunderts strebte nach der Veranschaulichung einer zeitlosen, ursprünglichen und unveränderlichen Schönheit, motiviert durch den Wunsch nach einer verlässlichen Aussage zur Welt, beseelt von dem Streben, vorzudringen zu den universellen Gesetzmäßigkeiten und ihnen einen gültigen Ausdruck zu verleihen. Diese Überzeugung hat Kandinsky, Mondrian und Malewitsch vorangetrieben. Max Bill beschäftigte sich ausgiebig mit der vielfältigen Wirkung des Quadrats. In zahlreichen Versionen – dynamisch, diszipliniert, konstruktiv – kehrt es immer wieder in seinen Werken. Im Quadrat gipfelt für Bill die Essenz der Geometrie an sich, der mathematischen Logik insgesamt. In den 1960er Jahren beschwören Donald Judd, Robert Morris, Sol Lewitt, Frank Stella und Carl Andre den „cube" als Paradigma der Gestaltung schlechthin, als reine, rationale, industrielle Metapher.⁷ Max Ackermann spricht von der „königlichen Geometrie" als Nektar der Kunst, die das Wesen der Dinge zum Klingen bringe.⁸ Es wäre ein Leichtes, diese Aufzählung fortzusetzen – in der Kunst.

⁶ Vgl. Hans Biedermann, *Simboli*, Mailand 2004.

⁷ Vgl. Gregor Stemmrich (Hrsg.), *Minimal Art. Eine kritische Retrospektive*, Dresden/Basel 1995, zum Beispiel S. 115ff.

cube.⁶ Throughout the history of philosophy, basic geometric forms have represented the perfect fusion of matter and spirit, the intermingling of space and time, which was an *a priori* given for Kant. Since Heraclitus, Aristotle and Plato, the process of abstraction has been manifest therein as the sum of man's knowledge and experience of his ontological condition. In art it is expressed as a non-representational picture or ornamental sign. We are familiar with Dürer's *Melancolia*, we know the doctrines of scale and proportion and the attempts made since antiquity to achieve objective proportion and mathematical correctness in planimetric drawing schemata. The square and the cube function as the essential tools in this context.

Abstraction in the 20th century strove to visualise a timeless, primal and unchanging beauty, motivated by a desire for a reliable statement on the world, informed by the endeavour to press forward to universals and to lend them valid expression. This was the conviction that drove Kandinsky, Mondrian and Malevich. Max Bill lavished a great deal of study on the manifold effects to be achieved with the square. In numerous versions – dynamic, disciplined and Constructive – it recurs again and again in his works. To Bill, the quintessence of geometry, the whole of mathematical logic, culminated in the square. In the 1960s Donald Judd, Robert Morris, Sol Lewitt, Frank Stella and Carl Andre invoked the "cube" as the very paradigm of design, as pure, rational, industrial metaphor.⁷ Max Ackermann speaks of "regal geometry" as the nectar of art which makes the essence of things resonate.⁸ It would be easy to continue with this enumeration – in art.

Looked at in this light, there are no parallels in jewellery, consequently no serial prefigurations of a mathematically grounded aesthetic in the narrower sense of the term; statements are lacking on geometric abstraction

⁶ Cf Hans Biedermann, *Simboli*, Milan 2004.

⁷ Cf Gregor Stemmrich (ed.), *Minimal Art. Eine kritische Retrospektive*, Dresden/Basel 1995, for instance pp.115ff.

 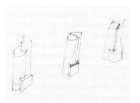

Im Schmuck gibt es, so gesehen, keine Parallele, folglich keine Ahnenreihe an Vorbildern für eine mathematisch fundierte Ästhetik im engeren Sinne, es fehlt an Äußerungen zur geometrischen Abstraktion, deren „Ornamentik" sich im Laufe der Zeit als „Pathosformeln", als „Bedeutungsmetaphern" in den Künsten etabliert hat. Und umgekehrt wurde ja der Anteil des zeitgenössischen Schmucks an der Konstituierung einer Kunst-Historie bislang noch gar nicht in Erwägung gezogen. Kodré jedoch stellt sich bewusst in einen solchen übergeordneten, die Bereiche miteinander verzahnenden Zusammenhang, rekrutiert gewissermaßen die künstlerische Zeichensprache, um sie für sein Sujet zu befruchten und zu funktionalisieren.

Es geht ihm um Regeln, es geht ihm aber auch um deren Infragestellung. Spontaneität und Expression gehen mit Rationalität, Berechnung und einem gewissen „Rappel à l'ordre" eine bildnerische Allianz ein, ein naturgemäßes Bündnis, denn, wie Mauro Corradini kürzlich in einem Katalog zur abstrakten Skulptur, zu einer Ausstellung, an der auch Helfried Kodré teilgenommen hat, festhielt: „L'arte non è solo un frutto spontaneo. Ma una ricerca guidata." (Die Kunst ist nicht nur ein spontanes Ergebnis, sondern auch eine überlegte, kontrollierte Forschung.)[9] Um Schmuck also in seinem Sinne zu bereichern und weiterzuentwickeln, hält sich Kodré von momentanen, flüchtigen Eingebungen fern und bekennt sich zu Inhalten, Gestaltungskriterien und Werten, die sich in der Vergangenheit behauptet haben und seit alters einen festen Platz einnehmen in der künstlerischen und philosophischen Recherche: die Erforschung und Vergegenständlichung von Raum durch die plastische Veranschaulichung seiner immanenten Bedingtheiten.

whose "decorative qualities" over time became established in the arts as "pathos formulas", as "metaphors for significance". And conversely, the part played by contemporary jewellery in constituting the history of art has not even been considered. Kodré, however, positions himself deliberately in a generic context of this kind that interlinks the fields, recruiting, in a certain sense, the artistic language of signs in order to fertilise it for his subject and make it functional.

He is concerned with rules but he is also concerned with questioning them. Spontaneity and expression have entered on a sculptural alliance with rationality, calculation and a certain "rappel à l'ordre", a natural alliance, since, as Mauro Corradini recently stated in a catalogue accompanying an exhibition of abstract sculpture: "L'arte non è solo un frutto spontaneo. Ma una ricerca guidata." (Art is not just a spontaneous result. But also controlled research.)[9] In order, therefore, to enrich jewellery as he understands it and develop it further on his terms, Kodré keeps his distance from momentary, fleeting brainstorms, professing allegiance instead to content, design criteria and values which proved their worth in the past and since antiquity have occupied a fixed position in artistic and philosophical research: exploring and objectifying space through rendering its inherent contingencies in sculptural terms.

[8] Vgl. Fritz Jacobi, „Geometrie als Gestalt – Die bildende Kunst im Spannungsfeld zwischen elementarer Form und konzeptueller Anschauung", in: *Geometrie als Gestalt. Strukturen der modernen Kunst von Albers bis Paik. Werke der Sammlung Daimler Chrysler*, Ausst.Kat., Berlin 1999, S. 10–35, Zitat S. 12.

[9] Mauro Corradini, „Attraversamenti: ritmi, misure e dismisure nella scultura astratta contemporanea", in: *Attraversamenti, Scultura Contemporanea*, Ausst Kat., Desenzano del Garda 2006, S. 8.

[8] Cf Fritz Jacobi, "Geometrie als Gestalt – Die bildende Kunst im Spannungsfeld zwischen elementarer Form und konzeptueller Anschauung", in: *Geometrie als Gestalt. Strukturen der modernen Kunst von Albers bis Paik. Werke der Sammlung Daimler Chrysler*, exhib. cat., Berlin 1999, pp. 10–35, quotation p. 12.

[9] Mauro Corradini, "Attraversamenti: ritmi, misure e dismisure nella scultura astratta contemporanea", in: *Attraversamenti, Scultura Contemporanea*, exhib. cat., Desenzano del Garda 2006, p. 8.

Skulptur/Sculpture, 2006

Wolfgang Prohaska

Zu Helfried Kodrés künstlerischer Physiognomie

Wer über einen lebenden Künstler schreibt, noch dazu über einen Freund, der einem über viele Jahre hinweg vertraut wurde, ist versucht, Objektivität und Abstand geringer zu achten und sich subjektiven Assoziationen zu überlassen, deren Verständlichkeit allerdings dann zur Disposition stünde. Das weiß der am besten, der im selben Metier gearbeitet hat wie der „Adressat" dieser Zeilen, nämlich im Metier des Schreibens oder Sprechens von oder über Kunstgeschichte. Doppelt „gefährdet" ist er, der Kunsthistoriker, sowieso schon, wenn er über die abgesicherten historischen Fakten oder zweifellose und konkrete Beobachtungen hinausgeht, den Bereich dessen verlässt, was mit (natur)wissenschaftlichen Methoden oder denen der Philologie untersucht werden kann. Ästhetisches Vergnügen sickert in die nüchterne, nachvollziehbare Beschreibung. Soll er aber nun alle Vertrautheit wegschieben, so tun als ob es sich bei den Broschen, Ringen, Spangen, „ziellosen" Objekten um Fremdes handelt, nicht um geliebten Schmuck, den er selbst Vertrauten geschenkt, den er an Freunden und Freundinnen, wenn nicht täglich, so doch vielfach gesehen, in der Hand gehalten hat, der ihm selbst geschenkt wurde… Das kann er nicht, dies bedeutete eine psychische Anstrengung, die dem Anlass des Schreibens, dem Künstler eine Art „Festschrift" zu widmen, nicht zu einem runden Geburtstag, aber vielleicht zu einem Punkt des Innehaltens, einem freudvollen Anlass also, zuwiderläuft. Leichtigkeit wäre demnach gefordert, etwas, was man in einer gewissen Widersinnigkeit vielleicht Wärme der Argumentation nennen könnte. Ich bekenne mich also zum Hedonismus, zur ästhetischen Freude, zum Genuss des Schauens: Es war nicht nur die Freude, etwas wieder gefunden zu haben, was ich verloren geglaubt hatte, als mir vor ein paar Monaten beim „Räumen" Kodrés runde, stählerne Manschettenknöpfe, sorgfältig in einem Säckchen aufbewahrt, wieder in die Hände fielen. Ich hatte sie wohl vor ca. 25 Jahren gekauft und sie waren „verschwunden", weil Hemden mit den genähten Manschetten-Schlitzen

Wolfgang Prohaska

An Artistic Profile of Helfried Kodré

Anyone who writes about a living artist, especially a friend of many years' standing, is tempted to pay less attention to objectivity and detachment and rely more on subjective associations – which, however, would then be subject to an arbitrary interpretation. No one is more aware of this than someone who has worked in the same field as the person these lines are "addressed" to, namely, that of writing on art history. As an art historian, he is in "double jeopardy" in any case when he goes beyond the assured historical facts, when he leaves the field of what can be investigated with the methods of science or philology. Aesthetic pleasure seeps into the sober, understandable description. However, should he thrust aside all familiarity, should he pretend that what matters about these brooches, rings, "purposeless" objects is that they are unrelated to him and not cherished jewellery he himself gives as presents, jewellery he has seen, if not daily, at least fairly often on his friends, jewellery he has held in his hand and which was also given to himself… This he cannot do; it would entail a mental strain which would contravene the occasion for writing this essay – dedicating a kind of *Festschrift* to the artist, not on a landmark birthday but perhaps at a moment for taking stock and an occasion to celebrate. This calls for a lighter touch, something that might paradoxically be called "friendly fire".

So I admit to hedonism, to aesthetic pleasure, to the sheer enjoyment of looking. It was not just the thrill of finding something I thought I had lost when a couple of months ago during a "clear-out" I came across a pair of Kodré's round steel cufflinks carefully stowed away in a little bag. I probably bought them about twenty-five years ago and they had "disappeared" because shirts with edged slits for cufflinks had gone out of fashion. I now wear shirts like this again and the pleasure I feel when I put the cufflinks on is hard to describe; austere double steel discs, wrought, like all his work, with the utmost precision and sporting a small cabochon ruby and a gold shaft – just to look at them and

Helfried Kodré, 1996

außer Gebrauch gekommen waren. Ich habe nun wieder solche Hemden, und meine Freude, die nüchternen, wie immer mit äußerster Präzision gearbeiteten, mit einem punktförmigen Rubin und einem goldenen Mittelstab versehenen Doppel-Stahlscheiben am Hemd zu montieren oder sie während des Essens, wenn die Manschetten aus dem Rockärmel schauen, zu betrachten, lässt sich schwer beschreiben: pure Freude an perfekt gelöster Formgelegenheit, Praktikabilität, Sicherheit des Sitzes, sozialer Stolz auch, ein so „schönes" Ding zu besitzen.

So verschieden auf den ersten Blick Kodrés Arbeiten der Frühzeit, sagen wir, bis zu seiner Abkehr von der Schmuckkunst Mitte der 70er Jahre von der Produktion der letzten 15 Jahre zu sein scheinen, so macht der kunsthistorisch in Wien beheimatete Beobachter die voraussehbare Entdeckung, dass, wie bei kaum jemandem in diesem Metier, die stilistische Wiedererkennbarkeit seiner Arbeiten hoch ist, „ein Kodré", sofern man einen gesehen, jenseits der offensichtlichen Verschiedenheiten leicht zu erkennen ist.

Vom „Spätwerk" her gesehen mögen die in den 60er Jahren in Zusammenarbeit mit Elisabeth Defner oder in Ateliergemeinschaft mit ihr entstandenen Stücke wie ein spielerisches Anknüpfen an sehr österreichische Traditionen aussehen, an die Tradition eines immer auch technisch virtuosen Naturalismus. Aber schon bald machten sich bei Kodrés Broschen etwa auch festere, rigidere Formen bemerkbar. Gleichsam geologische Schichtungen, Brüche, stoßen hart aneinander, fügen sich aber wieder ineinander, wie gebrochenes Glas oder Eis; in Broschen sind diese Bruchstücke aus Weißgold und Gelbgold vor eine Folie aus Stahl gesetzt, an den wenigen Treffpunkten der horizontal/vertikal verlaufenden Bruchlinien sind einzelne Steine, eine Goldader platziert (siehe Abb. unten links). An harte Weißgold-Silber-Bruchstücke eines „Halsbands" schmiegen sich am äußeren Rand irreguläre Nester aus kleinen Rubinen,

be aware of others looking at them during a meal when my cuffs proudly emerge from my jacket sleeves, sheer joy in the resolution of perfect form, practicality, secure fit – social prestige, too, in possessing and showing off such a "thing of beauty".

As different as Kodré's early work may seem at first sight from what he has produced in the past fifteen years until, broadly speaking, he abandoned art jewellery in the mid-1970s, an observer with art-historical roots in Vienna makes the predictable discovery that his style is highly recognisable, like hardly anyone else practising this craft; "a Kodré", once seen, is easy to identify, over and above the obvious differences.

From the aspect of his "late work", the pieces made in the 1960s in collaboration with Elisabeth Defner or in the studio they shared seem to allude playfully to very Austrian traditions, the tradition of a naturalism invariably based on technical virtuosity. But it was not long before sturdier, more rigid forms became noticeable in Kodré's brooches. Geological strata, as it were, faults and fissures collide at a sharp angle, only to fit together again, like broken glass or ice; in brooches these fragments of white or yellow gold are backed by a foil of steel; set in the few places where the fault lines merge horizontally/vertically are single stones, a vein of gold (see ill. down left). Irregularly shaped nests of little rubies, opals, diamonds cluster on the outer edge of the hard white gold-silver fragments of a "collar" (thus in a 1971 Kodré necklace, see ill. page 16), which in turn recall and link up with Defner's "magical-detailed hyperreality" or Sepp Schmölzer's work.

Kodré's "naturalism" was never charged biomorphically or animalistically as with Defner; his naturalism infiltrates the abstraction like an "irritation", which, however, has a positive implication – the colour of the stones is set as a sign of life. This is not the place to contrast Kodré with the animalist-esoteric material diversity of Elisabeth Defner, the

Brosche/Brooch, 1971

Opalen, Diamanten (so in einem Kollier Kodrés von 1971, siehe Abb. unten), die wieder an die „magisch-detaillierte Hyperrealität" Defners oder vorangehend an Sepp Schmölzers Arbeiten erinnern bzw. anknüpfen.

Kodrés „Naturalismus" war nie biomorph, animalistisch aufgeladen wie bei Defner, sein Naturalismus dringt in die Abstraktion ein wie eine „Störung", die gleichwohl positiv besetzt ist – die Farbe der Steine ist wie ein Lebenszeichen gesetzt. Hier ist nicht der Ort, die animalistisch-esoterische Materialvielfalt von Elisabeth Defner, der „Lehrerin" dieses Autodidakten, wenn es so was gibt, von diesem abzusetzen. (Er hat allerdings umgekehrt durch sein hohes Materialverständnis und seine technische Innovationsbegabung ihren ausufernden Biomorphismen zu Zeiten festere Struktur gegeben.) Dagegen bildete sich allmählich Strenge heraus, ein ganz spezifischer Minimalismus. Es hat wohl das Ausufernde, die Materialvielfalt, die esoterische Naturharmonie, den Naturalismus im genauen Wortsinn der Gegenseite – es sind auch die Abgusstechniken Defners gemeint – gebraucht, um Kodrés Gleichgewichtssinn, seine subtilen Materialsophismen zu formulieren und zu schärfen. Als Gegen-den-Strom-Schwimmer (manchmal sogar kohlhaasisch) hat sich Kodré gern selbst gefunden. Dasselbe gilt natürlich nicht nur für die Kunst Defners, sondern ebenso für die Materialexperimentierfreudigkeit vieler Schmuckkünstler, wie etwa eines Peter Skubic, um hier nur zwei der wichtigen Schmuckkünstler der 70er Jahre zu nennen. Kodrés Strenge trifft sich in den 70er Jahren mit den grazilen, jedoch linearereren Arbeiten Fritz Maierhofers.

Kodré hatte sich vor seiner von vielen bedauerten Abwendung von der Goldschmiedekunst um 1975 dem Abstraktionslevel, um es einmal grob zu formulieren, des Art Déco genähert (siehe Abb. unten rechts im Beitrag von Ellen Maurer Zilioli auf S. 7). Er mag, neben anderen Motiven, das *Dead End* zu diesem Zeitpunkt gefühlt haben. Er konnte mit den Theorie- und Material-Diskussionen, mit

"mentor" of this self-taught artist – if such a phenomenon exists. (Though conversely his thorough understanding of materials and his gift for technical innovation helped on occasion to give a firmer structure to her rampant biomorphisms.) In contrast, austerity has evolved gradually, a quite specific minimalism. Kodré most likely used the rampant aspect, the diversity of materials, the esoteric harmony with nature, the naturalism in a very literal sense of the verso aspect – this also refers to Defner's casting techniques – to formulate and hone the cutting edge of his poise, his subtle material sophistries. Like a swimmer against the tide, Kodré has managed to find himself. The same applies of course not only to Defner's art but just as much to the delight in material experimentation manifest in many makers of art jewellery, for instance someone like Peter Skubic, to name just two major jewellery artists of the 1970s. During this decade, Kodré's austerity dovetailed with the graceful yet linear work of Fritz Maierhofer.

Before abandoning goldsmithing – a step so many regretted – by around 1975 Kodré had approached the level of abstraction, roughly speaking, of Art Déco (see ill. down right in the essay by Ellen Maurer Zilioli on p. 7). Among other motives, he may have felt he had reached a dead end at that juncture. He probably felt little involvement in the discussions of the 1970s on theory and material, on the politicisation of jewellery-making. I remember Kodré visiting me in Munich – where I was working – in the mid-1970s, after a protracted break in our contact. Ten years previously, we had in fact studied art history together in Vienna, become friends, attended seminars together – I recall a memorable seminar on Romanesque wall painting taught by the celebrated Byzantine specialist Otto Demus; both of us read papers that were praised. Shortly after that, however, Kodré abandoned his study of art history to devote himself entirely to making jewellery. So we met in a Munich beer garden and talked – I was somewhat hesitant – about

Halsschmuck/Necklace, 1971

der Politisierung des Schmuck-Machens in den 70er Jahren wohl wenig anfangen. Ich erinnere mich, dass Kodré mich nach einer langen Unterbrechung unseres Kontaktes Mitte der 70er Jahre in München besuchte, wo ich damals arbeitete. Wir hatten ja zehn Jahre zuvor in Wien zusammen Kunstgeschichte studiert, uns angefreundet, zusammen Seminare besucht – ich erinnere mich an ein denkwürdiges über romanische Wandmalerei bei dem berühmten Byzantinisten Otto Demus, beide hatten wir gelobte Referate gehalten. Kurz danach hatte Kodré jedoch das Kunstgeschichtsstudium aufgegeben und sich ganz der Schmuckproduktion zugewendet. Wir trafen uns also in einem Münchener Biergarten und besprachen – ich auch tastend – sein Projekt: Er wollte nämlich mit der Kunstgeschichte wieder anfangen, die er zehn Jahre zuvor „abgegeben" hatte, um, wie gesagt, nur als Goldschmied zu arbeiten. Wie wir wissen, hatte er damit großen internationalen Erfolg gehabt. Ich freute mich zwar, dass er seinen Plan an diesem Scheidewege mit mir besprechen wollte, war mir aber – fremd in der Goldschmiede-Szene – auch über die ökonomischen Konsequenzen einer solchen Entscheidung, außer oberflächlich, nicht im Klaren. Nach meiner Übersiedlung nach Wien 1977 war der Freund schon wieder mitten im Studium. Dass er sich im Weiteren mit Architektur beschäftigen würde, konnte man sich vorstellen. In seiner brillanten Dissertation über den Stiegenhausbau öffentlicher Gebäude im 19. Jahrhundert bewährte sich sein Bedürfnis nach und seine Fähigkeit zur Abstraktion, Konstruktion, zur Durchleuchtung komplizierter, ineinander verschränkter Strukturen, schärfte sich sein perspektivischer Blick. Seine Lehrveranstaltungen über Mies van der Rohe, Le Corbusier etc. nach Abschluss der Dissertation waren gesucht, seine Erwartungen an die Studenten hoch, sie konnten gar nicht hoch genug sein, vielleicht waren sie in diesem Moment zu hoch, vielleicht war es auch nicht ganz einfach, sich im Alter von etwa Mitte 40 und als „gestandener" selbstbestimmter Künstler in die

his project: he wanted to return to the art history he had "given up" ten years ago in order, as said, to work solely as a goldsmith. As we know, this had brought him great international success. Although I was pleased that he wanted to talk his plan over with me at this critical juncture, I was an outsider on the goldsmith scene and was only superficially informed about the economic consequences of such a decision. After my move to Vienna in 1977, my friend was once again immersed in art history. I could imagine he would eventually move over to architectural studies. In his brilliant dissertation on staircase architecture in the nineteenth century, his need and aptitude for abstraction, construction, illumination of complex, interlocking structures honed his eye for perspective. The lectures and seminars he gave on Mies van der Rohe, Le Corbusier, et al. after he had finished his dissertation were very popular. He had high expectations of his students – they couldn't have been higher; perhaps they were too high at that particular moment; nor was it at all easy for someone in his mid-forties and an "old hand" as a self-determined artist to fit into the dependency-inducing structures of a hierarchically organised, career-orientated university organisation, and one which apart from this paid a pittance. In any case, to use the iconographic terms of art history, the "return of the prodigal son" to the artistic scene in the early 1990s was greeted with high expectations, and in 1996 Viennese art history would lose an exceptional teacher and independent spirit.

But how do you start all over again after a lapse of fifteen, twenty years to make new jewellery? It is harder and easier at the same time; not harder because of being out of practice, for Kodré had continued to do his precision finger exercises, had honed his technical skills, but had largely abstained from creating works of his own. Although the discussions and disputes over trends in the 1970s and 1980s – mostly dead-end – had not entirely passed him by (he observed the scene attentively and critically from a

Abhängigkeiten produzierenden Strukturen eines hierarchisch organisierten, karriereorientierten Universitätsbetriebes zu fügen, in dem man noch dazu erbärmlich wenig verdiente. Jedenfalls wurde Anfang der 90er Jahre die „Rückkehr des verlorenen Sohnes" zur künstlerischen Tätigkeit, um es kunsthistorisch-ikonographisch auszudrücken, in der Szene mit hohen Erwartungen begrüßt – und die Wiener Kunstgeschichte sollte 1996 einen vorzüglichen Lehrer und unabhängigen Geist verlieren.

Aber wie fängt man nach 15, 20 Jahren wieder an, neuen Schmuck zu machen? Es ist schwerer und leichter zugleich, schwerer nicht, weil man aus der Übung gekommen war, Kodré hatte weiterhin seine Präzisions-Fingerübungen gemacht, seine technischen Fertigkeiten geschärft, sich aber der Eigenschöpfungen weitgehend enthalten. Dafür sind an ihm aber die späterhin sackgassenartig verlaufenen Diskussions- und Richtungsstreitigkeiten der 70er und 80er Jahre zwar nicht vorbeigegangen (weil er natürlich die Szene aufmerksam und kritisch aus seiner Distanz beobachtet hat), hatten ihn aber wohl nicht wirklich berührt: ob man – und das war in der kapitalismuskritischen Zeit in den 70ern ein Thema – Gold oder Edelsteine verwenden dürfe, welche Materialien überhaupt brauchbar seien, ob Schmuck überhaupt „Kunst" sei; die Diskussionen des Werk- und Funktionsbegriffs, über die Tragbarkeit, die Tragnotwendigkeit des Schmuck-Objekts. Er hat sich in einem kurzen ironisch fragenden, ideologie- und dogmenkritischen Statement [1] dazu bekannt, dass es ihm 2003 unter den Voraussetzungen des wiedergewonnen freien Marktes leichter falle und dass es für ihn weniger frustrierend sei, nun Schmuck zu machen als in den ideologisch kämpfenden, intoleranten, rechthaberischen 70er und 80er Jahren. Er mahnt zur Bescheidenheit, warnt davor, Schmuck inhaltlich zu überfrachten, da das Verhältnis von ideologischer Aussage und praktischer

[1] Helfried Kodré, „Nouvelle Cuisine – oder zurück an den Anfang. Die Schmuckkunst-Szene der 1970er Jahre", in: *Re-view. Aspekte Österreichischer Schmuckkunst*, Ausst.Kat., Wien 2003.

distance), they had not really touched him either: whether an artist – and this was a contentious issue in the anti-capitalist 1970s – ought to use gold or precious stones; which materials were at all permissible; whether jewellery was "art" at all; then there were the discussions about the work and function concept, wearability; how necessary is it to wear an object of decorative jewellery? He admitted in a brief, ironically questioning statement[1] critical of both ideology and dogma that it was easier for him and less frustrating to make jewellery then in 2003 under the conditions of the re-established free market than during the ideological battles of the intolerant, self-righteous 1970s and 1980s. He urged restraint, warning against overloading jewellery with content since the relationship between ideological statement and its translation into practice only made the limitations of jewellery as a medium all the more apparent.

Freed of having to search around for "politically correct" materials, Kodré has, if you like, taken the reductionist route: he is again working in such traditional materials as gold, silver, steel, copper, where he sometimes roughens the surfaces so that subtle interrelationships emerge under the play of light. He scarcely works with stones, rather with "base" polychrome materials or glass when he wishes to achieve colour effects over and above the various metal colours.

Kodré's earlier brooches were characterised by the explosive rift of an irritation into a smooth surface, the opposition between exalted uniformity and intricate detail produced by stone or splintered stone – simultaneously freedom and bonding. However, since the 1990s and his abandonment of art history, he has reduced the overall form. His brooches, also his ear jewellery, for instance, have become rod-shaped or cylindrical; the irritations and

[1] Helfried Kodré, „Nouvelle Cuisine – oder zurück an den Anfang. Die Schmuckkunst-Szene der 1970er Jahre", in: *Re-view. Aspekte Österreichischer Schmuckkunst*, exhib. cat., Vienna 2003.

Umsetzung nur die Grenzen des Mediums Schmuck umso deutlicher werden lässt. Befreit davon, „auf der Straße" nach neuen Materialien zu suchen, geht Kodré einen, wenn man so will, reduktionistischen Weg: Er arbeitet weiter in den traditionellen Materialien Gold, Silber, Stahl, Kupfer, deren Oberflächen er manchmal aufraut, damit im Licht differenzierte Verhältnisse entstehen, kaum mit Steinen, eher mit "unedlen" bunten Materialien oder Glas, wenn er jenseits der verschiedenen Metallfarben Farbeffekte erzielen will.

War in Kodrés frühen Broschen der explosionsartige Einbruch einer Störung in eine glatte Fläche, der Gegensatz von hoher Einheitlichkeit und durch Stein bzw. Steinsplitter produzierter Kleinteiligkeit – die Gleichzeitigkeit von Freiheit und Bindung – ein charakteristisches Merkmal, so reduziert er seit den 90er Jahren, seit seiner Abkehr von der Kunstgeschichte, die Gesamtform. Seine Broschen, auch Ohrschmuckstücke, z.B. werden stabförmig oder runden sich zylinderartig, die Störungen – und (Ver)Störungen sind durchgehendes Merkmal seiner Schmuckkunst – entstehen durch Brechung der Vertikalen oder Horizontalen mittels verquer eingeschobener, geometrisch einfacher Kreissegmente oder Dreiecke, die aus farblich verschiedenen Metallen gearbeitet sind; auch hart aneinander stoßende, mehrteilige plastische Gebilde entstehen – hier finden sich die Ansätze zur – wiewohl immer tragbar am Körper – freien abstrakten Skulptur. Seine Fingerringe, scheinbar anorganisch viereckig im Aufriss, mit spitzen oder gebrochenen, gegeneinander verschobenen Aufsätzen versehen, schmiegen sich nicht mehr an den Finger, sondern betonen ihre Selbstständigkeit. Andererseits greift Kodré gerade bei Ohrschmuck auf Lösungen zurück, die die Biegsamkeit des Metalls und damit Rundung und Anschmiegsamkeit vermitteln.

In den letzten Jahren macht sich bei Kodré eine Tendenz bemerkbar, die man mit Verräumlichung (und zwar überra-

dissonances have been a consistent feature of his art; they arise by disrupting verticals or horizontals through geometrically simple circle segments or triangles thrust in laterally and worked of polychrome metals; we also see multipart sculptural configurations set at harsh angles to each other – the beginnings of free abstract sculpture, nonetheless always wearable on the body. His finger rings, inorganically angular when viewed in elevation, with pointed or broken, staggered mounts, no longer snuggle on the finger but emphasise its independence. Meanwhile, especially in ear jewellery, Kodré reverts to solutions that convey the ductility of the metal and thus undulation and smooth fit.

In recent years, a tendency has become noticeable in Kodré's work which we could describe as an extension into spatiality, for instance the ear jewellery, and this relates, surprisingly, not only to reality but also to illusion and perspective. Here, too, the development is both potential and real in the direction of sculpture existing in space. The illusionist character of elements consisting of various little metal plates layered at disparate angles with surfaces partly roughened by hatched engravings derives from the way the metal at the edges seems to fold over like paper. The effect is like that of a *trompe l'oeil*, as if the observer is confronted with a still life composed of staggered, layered sheets of paper. Creating real space are constructions of tiered square or rectangular metal frames of silver or gold at complex disparate angles, seemingly inserted into one another on pins, which support the "body" of a brooch, or – in a row – form the links of a necklace, or which may even grow into free-standing sculptures. The great charm of these configurations is their multifaceted points of view, their form shifting kaleidoscope-like at every angle, the astounding virtuosity of the sculpture's concept, which of

schender Weise sowohl illusionistisch-perspektivisch als auch real) bezeichnen könnte – auch hier potentiell und real die Entwicklung zur im Raum bestehenden Skulptur. Illusionistisch ist bei den aus unterschiedlichen Metallplättchen gegeneinander geschichteten und oberflächlich z.T. mit gestrichelten Gravuren aufgerauten Elementen das scheinbare Umklappen von Ecken, als ob Metall umbrechbar wäre. Es ergibt sich gleichsam ein *Trompe l'oeil*-Effekt, als ob der Betrachter ein Stillleben aus verschoben aufeinander geschichteten Papierblättern vor sich hätte. Realen Raum schaffend sind Konstruktionen kompliziert gegeneinander verwinkelter, scheinbar ineinander gesteckter, aufgetürmter viereckiger Metallrahmen aus Silber oder Gold, die die „Körper" von Anstecknadeln oder – aneinander gereiht – die Glieder von Halsketten bilden, aber auch zu frei stehenden Skulpturen wachsen können. Der eminente Reiz dieser Gebilde ist ihre Vielansichtigkeit, ihre sich aus jedem Blickwinkel kaleidoskopartig verändernde Gestalt, die verblüffende Virtuosität des Konzepts dieser Skulptur, die natürlich genaue Konstruktionszeichnungen voraussetzt. Der Künstler Kodré setzt – so würde der Kunsthistoriker sagen – seinen *Disegno interno*, seine abstrakte Idee, in reale Architektur, in plastische Form um.

Kodrés Weg als Schmuckkünstler ist, wie auch seine Biografie, gebrochen in zyklisch wiederkehrende Ab- und Zuwendungen von und zu seiner „Berufung", seinen Berufungen, wenn man so will, denn, aus welchen Gründen auch immer, der künstlerische Impetus brach sich zu Zeiten am Analysierenden, Nachschaffenden des Kunsthistorikers, zu dem es ihn immer wieder trieb. So sind auch seine Äußerungen zur eigenen Kunst gebrochen, distanziert. Gutes Beispiel sein schon erwähntes ironisch gefärbtes Statement zur Schmuckkunst-Szene der 1970er „Nouvelle Cuisine – oder zurück an den Anfang", *ex post* und histori-

course presupposes precise construction drawings. Kodré the artist transports – as the art historian would put it – his *disegno interno*, his abstract idea, into real architecture, into sculptural form.

The path Kodré has taken as a jewellery artist is like his biography, broken up into a cyclically recurring hither and thither as regards his "vocation" – indeed, his vocations. Whatever the reason, the creative impetus fractured on colliding with the analytic and reproductive function of the art historian, a calling that has exercised its pull on him time and again. Hence his statements on his own art are also fractured, detached. A good example of this is the ironically tinged statement he made on the 1970s art jewellery scene, which I mentioned above: "Nouvelle Cuisine – oder zurück an den Anfang" ("Nouvelle Cuisine – or Back to Square One"), *ex post facto* and historicising; then there is the other statement, probably cryptic, "unintelligible" to some readers, in the exhibition catalogue *turning-point – schmuck aus österreich zur jahrtausendwende* [2], where, without further commentary, he quotes from a handbook of tennis technique on the swinging movement needed to create "forehand top spin". But to understand this you have to realise that Kodré is an enthusiastic, occasionally even manic tennis player with a thorough grounding in the theory of the game. The text from the handbook is written at a high technical level, with only a sprinkling of colloquial expressions such as the need for a "quick hand" in the swing-out movement or a "feeling for timing in motion". It is the description of an utterly physical process, at the same time at such a high level of abstraction, inconceivably abstract, that it remains inaccessible to the uninitiated. Can we imagine Kodré thus as a teacher in an art history seminar? Probably not. But the "metaphor" cited above probably conceals something else; otherwise such a self-

[2] Susanne Hammer, Fritz Maierhofer (Hrsg.), *turning-point – schmuck aus österreich zur jahrtausendwende*, exhib. cat., Vienna 1999.

sierend, oder das andere, manchen Leser wohl verrätselt zurücklassende, „unverständliche" im Ausstellungskatalog *turning-point – schmuck aus österreich zur jahrtausendwende*[2], wo er ohne weiteren Kommentar aus einem Handbuch der Tennistechnik zur Ausholbewegung beim „Vorhand Topspin" zitiert. Dazu muss man allerdings wissen, dass Kodré ein begeisterter, zu Zeiten manischer, auch theoretisch einschlägig überaus versierter Tennisspieler ist. In den Text aus dem Handbuch, der auf einem hohen technizistischen Level geschrieben ist, sind nur wenige gleichsam kolloquiale Floskeln wie die „schnelle Hand" beim Ausholen oder das „Gefühl für das timing der Bewegung" eingestreut. Es ist die Beschreibung eines eminent physischen Vorgangs, die gleichzeitig auf einem so hohen Abstraktionsniveau steht, bis zur Unvorstellbarkeit abstrakt ist, dass sie für einen nicht Eingeweihten unverständlich bleibt. Kann man sich so den Pädagogen Kodré beim Kunstgeschichtsunterricht vorstellen? Wohl nicht. Aber in der zitierten „Metapher" steckt wohl etwas anderes, sonst hätte sich ein so bewusster Künstler wie er diesen Text kaum ausgesucht. Ich glaube, es steckt etwas zur Widersprüchlichkeit, zu den Antagonismen von Kodrés Kunst darin. Der Text zum Topspin und zur Ausholbewegung führt die hohe, gleichsam geometrische Berechenbarkeit des Vorgangs vor und nimmt gleichzeitig in der Abstraktion der Formulierung die Körperlichkeit des „Schlags" zurück. Irre ich nicht gravierend, so spannt sich zwischen diesen Polen ein wichtiger abbildender Teil von Kodrés Werk. Es ist schade, dass es zu einer anderen, noch persönlicheren Idiosynkrasie Kodrés – und er hat einige, immer auch ironisch „beschlagen", zu bieten – wie zu seiner tief sitzenden Abneigung gegen Hunde keinen vergleichbar einsichtigen, autoanalytischen Text gibt. Ich würde dem aber in keiner Weise vorgreifen wollen.

aware artist would hardly have chosen that particular text. I believe it contains something of the contradictions, the antagonisms in Kodré's art. The text on top spin and swinging motion presents as it were the same high degree of geometric calculability of a process, meanwhile reducing the physicality of the "stroke" by formulating it in abstract terms. If I am not gravely mistaken, the charged field between these poles forms an important visual aspect of Kodré's work. Sadly, no comparably illuminating, self-analytical text exists that applies to another, even more personal idiosyncrasy of Kodré's – and he has several, but always tinged with irony – for instance his deep-seated dislike of dogs. And I would in no way wish to take a pre-emptive shot at writing it.

[2] Susanne Hammer, Fritz Maierhofer (Hrsg.), *turning-point – schmuck aus österreich zur jahrtausendwende*, Ausst.Kat., Wien 1999.

Karl Bollmann
Why Jewellery? – An Essay

"Thus all things seek their own paths, All feel the joys of returning. That only remains in the eternal order, Which the beginning unites with the end, Which closes to a fixed circle." (Boethius[1])

"M'illumino d'immenso" – *"I illumine myself with the immeasurable"* (Giuseppe Ungaretti, 26.1.1917[2])

Helfried Kodré must have had every reason to feel satisfaction in 1975. By then he mastered the goldsmith's craft – art as skill in configuring matter but also as the ability to make one's innermost and leading-edge aesthetic ideas visible and experienceable. His position as a front runner among artists had not only been sealed by his having participated in numerous exhibitions and having received awards; he had also been ranked by Karl Schollmayer, a leading organiser and theorist of the "jewellery as art"-scene, in his work *Neuer Schmuck* in the category of the "arrived". He was, therefore, already more mature than the group comprising the "young generation". Helfried Kodré discovered one of his works on the jacket of this essential standard work (see ill. below). Schollmayer's evaluation of Kodré's work was that his pieces not only ranked with the best of the Secession and the Wiener Werkstätten but even surpassed them. He concluded that Kodré's great contribution, as important as it was gratifying, to the new jewellery and that of Austria in particular, would exert a lasting influence. His works were being sold worldwide and did especially well on the Viennese society market.

Despite all these propitious signs and circumstances, Kodré ended – and at that time it seemed for good – his activity as an artist in 1975. He resumed the university studies he had dropped out of, took his doctorate and then began to teach art history at Vienna University. As an academic, he also delved into the depths. The excursions he led to the Palladio villas are still raved about in broad circles

---

[1] Boethius, "Trost der Philosophie" (The Consolations of Philosophy), 524 AD, 3rd book, 2.C 34 – 38, from: *Bibliothek der Antike*, Munich 1991, p. 116.

[2] Giuseppe Ungaretti, *Gedichte*, Frankfurt 1961, pp. 6f.

Brosche/Brooch, 1967/68

Wien. Auch als Wissenschaftler ist er in die Tiefe gegangen. Über seine Exkursionen zu den Palladio-Villen wird noch heute in weiten Kreisen kunsthistorisch Interessierter enthusiastisch berichtet. Es mag sein, dass sich im Laufe der Jahre eine gewisse Enttäuschung über die Geringfügigkeit der Möglichkeit ergab, eine lustlose Studentenmenge zu wissenschaftlicher Selbsttätigkeit heranzuführen.

Trägerinnen von Kodré-Schmuck sind diesem verbunden, ein Leben lang. Die Physis verändert sich mehr als die Psyche. Helfried Kodré wurde im Jahre 1990 gebeten, einen seiner Armreife aus alter Zeit zu erweitern. Nach den ästhetischen Überzeugungen Kodrés war dies unmöglich; eine Lösung bestand einfach darin, einen neuen Armreif zu machen (siehe Abb. unten links und Abb. 1, S. 34). Der Reiz der Aufgabenstellung, ihre Bewältigung und die Lust an der Erzeugung machten etwas manifest: Wenn Helfried Kodré sich selbst gemäß leben wollte, so musste er wieder Schmuck machen. Ein Talent ist eine Verpflichtung. Helfried Kodré hat sich ihr ohne lange Überlegung gestellt.

Seine neuen Arbeiten waren keine Wiederholung oder auch nur Fortsetzung – im Sinne einer Anstückelung – dessen, was er vor mehr als einem Jahrzehnt beendet hatte. Dies wäre nicht wahrhaft gewesen. Wenn es Qualität in der Kunst gibt, so waren die neuen Arbeiten besser und damit wesentlicher als die der Frühzeit. Gegen jede vernunftgemäße Erwartung war jedoch der Weg zum äußeren Erfolg mühselig und entbehrungsreich. Die Strahlkraft und Gültigkeit seiner Arbeiten wurde anfangs kaum wahrgenommen.

Lässt sich dies erklären?

Heute wie damals bestimmt eine Überlegung Kodrés gesamtes Schmuckschaffen: Wie wird das Schmuckstück aussehen, wenn es getragen wird, und kann ich es dann verantworten?

In der Zeit der ersten Schaffensperiode des Helfried Kodré schien aber gerade dies seinen revolutionären Kollegen

of art history buffs. It may well be that over the years arose a certain degree of disappointment at the lack of possibilities for leading an apathetic pack of students to academic independence.

Women who wear Kodré jewellery remain attached to it all their lives. The body changes more than the psyche. Helfried Kodré was asked in 1990 to widen one of his bangles from way back. According to Kodré's aesthetic conviction, that would have been impossible; the just solution was arrived at of making a new bangle (see ill. down left and ill. 1, p. 34). The attractiveness of the task, of accomplishing it, and the pleasure felt in creating made something clear: if Helfried Kodré wanted to live by his own standards, he would have to make jewellery again. Talent confers an obligation. Without mulling it over for very long, Helfried Kodré accepted it.

His new works did not constitute replication or even continuation – in the paratactic sense – of what he had ended more than a decade before. That would not have been true to his principles. If there is such a thing as quality in art, the new works were better and, therefore, more essential than those of his early years. Against all reasonable expectations, however, the way to extrinsic success was arduous and full of hardships. The brilliance and validity of his works was at first hardly noticed.

Is there an explanation for this?

Today a thought of Kodré's informs his entire work in jewellery just as it did then: what will the piece of jewellery look like when it is worn and can I justify it then?

In Helfried Kodré's first creative period, this in particular did not seem especially important to his revolutionary colleagues. The buzzword binding on the revolutionary group was the dogma "jewellery is art" – so that joining the art debate raging at the time seemed unavoidable. Is art the excrement (the product) of the artist or is rather the activity

Armband / Bracelet, 1971 / 72

nicht so besonders wichtig. In der revolutionären Gruppe war das Dogma „Schmuck ist Kunst" ausgegeben – womit auch eine Einschaltung in die damalige Kunstdebatte unausbleiblich schien. Ist Kunst die Ausscheidung (das Produkt) des Künstlers oder ist überhaupt die Tätigkeit eines jeden Menschen Kunst? Entsteht Kunst überhaupt nur in der Debatte darüber, was Kunst ist?

Es schien Helfried Kodré, dass er mit seinen Grundsätzen nicht in der Gruppe arbeiten konnte. Um jedoch alleine zu bleiben, fehlte ihm zunächst die Gelassenheit.

Bei seiner Rückkehr waren die Schmuckkünstler längst nicht mehr so theoriesüchtig. Aber ein Heimkehrer hat in Europa schon seit langer Zeit keinen Anspruch auf Begeisterung. Nunmehr erwartete das Publikum von dem vermeintlich an der Universität mit wissenschaftlichen Begründungen aufgeladenen Künstler Helfried Kodré ein mächtiges Wort der Aufklärung. Dieser aber empfand sogar schon Fragen von Galeristinnen vor Kunstinteressierten nach seinen Gedanken zur Arbeit als unangebracht und widerwärtig. Als anlässlich eines Sammelkatalogs österreichischer Schmuckkünstler zum Jahre 2000 der Aufruf erging, jeder möge ein seine Arbeit erläuterndes Statement verfassen, setzte er ohne weitere Erklärung die minutiöse Darstellung des „Vorhand Topspin – die Ausholbewegung" aus einem Tennislehrbuch als Zitat ein. Um das Maß voll zu machen, schrieb seine Frau Eva Kodré-Klingenstein im selben Katalog[3] an anderer Stelle einen Aufsatz mit dem Titel „Mach' mich schön", obwohl doch jeder rechtschaffene Kunstbeflissene wusste, dass Kunst bei sonstiger Verwerfung zweckfrei zu sein hat, das Wort „schön" nicht auszusprechen ist und damit der Mief ästhetischer Süßlichkeit die geistigen Höhen umdampfte. Beide waren der Auffassung, dass ein einfaches Hinsehen auf die Arbeiten derartige Missver-

engaged in by everyone art? Does art emerge only in the debate about what art is?

It seemed to Helfried Kodré that, with his principles, he could not work in the group. However, he at first lacked the composure to remain on his own.

On his return, he found the jewellery artists not nearly as addicted to theory as they had been. But he who returns from exile long had no claim to enthusiasm in Europe for quite some time. Now the public expected a powerful statement of enlightenment from the artist Helfried Kodré since he was presumed to have been charged up with academic explanations at the university. He, on the other hand, found even the questions about his thoughts on his work asked in front of an audience of art aficionados by ladies who ran galleries inappropriate and repellent. When a catalogue surveying the work of Austrian jewellery artists was being compiled in 2000 and everyone was requested to compose a statement explaining his work, Kodré contributed, without further explanation, a detailed representation of "forehand top spin – the movement of reaching out" quoted from a tennis instruction book. If that were not enough, his wife, Eva Kodré-Klingenstein, contributed to the same catalogue[3] an essay entitled "Mach' mich schön" ("Make me beautiful") as if every self-respecting culture vulture didn't know that art had to be without a purpose; in the midst of all the commotion made about it, the word "beautiful" was not to be uttered and with it the miasma of a cloying aestheticism fogged the pinnacles of the intellect. Both Kodrés were of the opinion that simply looking at the works would prevent such misconceptions from arising, quite the contrary in fact.

However, a substantial part of the problem rests in the status of jewellery within our culture. What is jewellery? Is jewellery the freely chosen object of self-determination,

[3] Susanne Hammer, Fritz Maierhofer (Hrsg.), *turning-point – schmuck aus österreich zur jahrtausendwende*, Ausst.Kat., Wien 1999.

[3] Susanne Hammer, Fritz Maierhofer (Hrsg.), *turning-point – schmuck aus österreich zur jahrtausendwende*, exhib. cat., Vienna 1999.

Kette/Necklace, 1999,
Privatsammlung Österreich/private collection Austria

ständnisse erst gar nicht aufkommen lassen könnte, ganz im Gegenteil.

Ein wesentlicher Teil des Problems liegt jedoch in der Stellung des Schmuckes innerhalb unserer Kultur. Was ist Schmuck? Ist Schmuck der frei gewählte Gegenstand zur Selbstbestimmung, seine Auswahl und sein Tragen ein lustvolles Tun für sich selbst und andere, eine Einladung zum Fest des Lebens? Oder ein mit allen Gattungen des Aberglaubens und der Schwärmerei verträglicher Schaum, mit dem man die schönsten Blasen werfen und sich dahinter verbergen kann, um die anderen damit zu betrügen? (in Anlehnung an F.H. Jacobi, „Über einen gewissen Schaum von Spinozismus", 1785) Ist Schmuck eine prometheische Präpotenz? Oder gilt das, was Boethius im „Trost der Philosophie", 524 n.C., sagt:

„Denn den anderen Lebewesen ist, sich nicht zu kennen, Natur; den Menschen ist es als Verdorbenheit anzurechnen. Wieweit erstreckt sich dieser euer Irrtum, wenn ihr glaubt, dass sich etwas durch fremden Schmuck schmücken lasse! Dies ist doch unmöglich; denn wenn etwas durch ein Beiwerk strahlt, dann liebt man zwar das Beiwerk, was aber davon verdeckt und verhüllt wird, verharrt in seiner dadurch um nichts geminderten Hässlichkeit." [4]

Ist Schmuck der Rest einer primitiven anthropologischen Stufe, der dort ruhig zurückbleiben soll, weil er das Kulturprogramm der Menschheit hindern könnte, die Veredelung durch Vergeistigung zu erreichen?

Alle diese Fragen stellen sich den Superreichen nicht und auch nicht jenen, denen Kultur nichts bedeutet oder die in einer festgefügten Ordnung – einem Ordenshaus – stehen.[5]

Die Schmuckkünstler produzieren für alle, aber sie brauchen die Kulturträger, die Meinungsmacher, die wissen, wie die Glückseligkeit auf Erden auch ohne Berufung auf eine Religion zu erreichen ist. Diese Schicht – die

[4] Boethius, „Trost der Philosophie", 524 n.C., 2. Buch, 5 P. 101–106, aus: *Bibliothek der Antike*, München 1991, S. 101.

[5] Die Ablehnung des Schmucks durch die abrahamitischen Religionen, aber auch schon durch die Hochkultur der Griechen, ist klar und nicht weiter zu diskutieren: Die Herstellung einer Sache, die den Menschen als Mensch bestätigt, erscheint ohne Solennisierung durch einen Priester als unbedingt teuflisch.

choosing and wearing it an activity pleasurable to oneself and others, an invitation to the feast of life? Or frothy suds compatible with all genres of superstition and fanatical rapture with which one can blow the most beautiful bubbles and conceal oneself behind them in order to deceive others? (here a debt is owed to F.H. Jacobi, "Über einen gewissen Schaum von Spinozismus", 1785) Is jewellery promethean prepotence? Or is what Boethius says in "The Consolations of Philosophy", 524 AD, true:

"For other creatures it is Nature not to know themselves; in human beings it is to be considered depravity. How far extends this, your error, if you believe that something can adorn itself with alien adornment! That is impossible, after all; for if something shines by virtue of accessories, one may love the accessories but what is hidden and veiled by them persists in a hideousness that has not been reduced one jot." [4]

Is jewellery the relic of a primitive anthropological level, one that definitely should stay there because it could hamper humanity's cultural agenda of attaining nobility through spiritualisation?

All these questions are not asked by the superrich or those to whom culture means nothing or those caught up in a rigid order – a monastic establishment.[5]

Jewellery artists produce for everyone but they need the pillars of the cultural establishment, the shapers of public opinion, who know how happiness is to be achieved on earth without the need for professing a religion. This class – the "intellectuals" – has learned to plan according to the dictates of utilitarianism and risk minimisation. Security before beauty! In their rejection of jewellery they probably feel superior, even in respect of the traditional ethical components, according to which chests of jewellery are placed by the Devil at the disposal of an elderly man so he

[4] Boethius, "Trost der Philosophie" (The Consolations of Philosphy), 524 AD, 2nd book, 5 P. 101–106, from: *Bibliothek der Antike*, Munich 1991, p. 101.

[5] The rejection of jewellery by the Abrahamic religions as well as the civilisation of ancient Greece is obvious and needs no further discussion: making something which confirms man's humanity appears entirely the work of the Devil without clerical sanction.

„Intellektuellen" – hat gelernt, nach Zweckmäßigkeit und Risikominimierung zu planen. Sicherheit vor Schönheit! In ihrer Ablehnung von Schmuck dürfen sie sich überlegen fühlen, auch in Hinblick auf die traditionelle ethische Komponente, wonach Schmuck dem alternden Mann kästchenweise vom Teufel zur Verfügung gestellt wird, um die blonde Unschuld zu verführen (*Faust, der Tragödie erster Teil*). Der Reiz vergeht, und am Ende lädt Schmuck doch zum Denken ein. Lässt sich alles Unschöne leichter denken als alles Schöne?

Für den Schmuck gilt nicht das Leid des Paul Klee „Denn uns trägt kein Volk", sondern „Denn uns tragen keine Intellektuellen". Die Kennerschaft fehlt.

Wie konnte es Helfried Kodré gelingen – wenn auch nach Jahren – sich letztlich doch durchzusetzen – und das auch bei Intellektuellen?

Schmuckkünstlern und ihrem Schmuck muss eines gemeinsam sein – Beharrlichkeit. Wenn Kunst mehr sein soll als ein substanzlos-begeistertes Strömen des Geistes und wenn die Mitteilbarkeit der menschlichen Empfindungen als möglich angenommen wird, weil gerade dies den Menschen zum Menschen macht, so muss die Mitteilung dingfest zu machen sein. Sie muss in einem Gegenstand liegen, der Substanz hat, also beharrlich ist. Dingfest bedeutet aber auch, dass der Gegenstand die Empfindung ohne weiteres mitteilt, also unmittelbar, spontan aus der Sache heraus, primär ohne Sekundärdoktrin.

Schmuck ist romantisch.

Zunächst geht es um den Schmuck als solchen. Ein Kunsthistoriker steht zur Vergangenheit, sei sie die der Menschheit überhaupt oder seine eigene. Die Rückkehr zeigt zunächst, dass es kein Ende und keine Überwindung von Ideen gibt, sondern nur ein Weiterarbeiten an der Bestimmung des Menschen – und dazu gehört auch wesentlich die Idee des Schmucks.

can seduce the innocent blonde maiden (*Faust: The First Part of the Tragedy*). The charm is lost and ultimately jewellery does, after all, invite one to think. Is it easier to think about everything that is ugly and evil than about everything that is beautiful?

The anguish of a Paul Klee "for no people supports us" does not apply to jewellery, rather "for no intellectuals know or wear us". Connoisseurship is lacking.

How could Helfried Kodré ultimately succeed – even many years later – in asserting himself – and do so with intellectuals as well?

Jewellery artists and their jewellery must have one thing in common – persistence. If art is to be more than an enthusiastic flux of spirit without substance and if it is accepted that human feelings can be imparted just because this is what makes a creature human, the message must be apprehensible. It must lie in an object which has substance, that is, persists. Apprehensible, however, also means that the object must impart the feeling without further ado, that is immediately, spontaneously arising from the thing itself, primarily without being seconded by doctrine.

Jewellery is romantic.

First of all, what is at stake is jewellery as such. An art historian relies on the past, be it mankind's or his own. Reversion to the past shows first of all that there is no end to ideas and no overcoming them but rather working further on the destination of man – and the idea of jewellery is also an essential part of this.

According to K.W.F. Solger, "the collective consciousness (strives) through a sort of instinct to attain the beautiful by seeking to order gradually the conditions of its own existence according to the idea. From this grows the love of jewellery and adornment, which also has a noble source in ordinary life. What is noble in the desire for jewellery is the intimation that the beautiful might be

Laut K.W.F. Solger strebt „das gemeine Bewusstsein ... durch eine Art Instinct dahin, das Schöne dadurch zu erlangen, dass es die Bedingungen seines eigenen Daseins nach und nach der Idee gemäß zu ordnen sucht. Daraus entsteht die Liebe zum Schmuck und Zierrath, der auch im gemeinen Leben eine edle Quelle hat. Das Edle, welches in dem Verlangen nach Schmucke liegt, ist die Ahndung, dass sich das Schöne mit dem gemeinen Leben versöhnen könne. Die Abneigung gegen den Schmuck führt zur offenbaren Barbarei".[6]

Schelling, Hegel und Hölderlin schreiben in ihrer Gemeinschaftsarbeit, dem so genannten „Ältesten Systemprogramm": „Ich bin nun überzeugt, dass der höchste Akt der Vernunft, der, indem sie alle Ideen umfasst, ein ästhetischer Akt ist, und dass Wahrheit und Güte nur in der Schönheit verschwistert sind." Stimmt dies, so hat Helfried Kodré Recht: Es wäre unvernünftig, auch nur den Ansatz einer Erklärung zu geben.

Sicher klingt dies nach unerreichbaren Idealen; aber ein Gutteil des besseren Lebens liegt eben darin, die Erleuchtung durch Ideale zu suchen.

Die Genietheoretiker und die Sinnenmechaniker sind sich aber in einem völlig einig: Es geht letztlich immer um die Freiheit des Menschen. Insoweit macht es auch keinen Unterschied, ob man der Theorie anhängt, dass alles Kunst ist, was ein Künstler von sich gibt, oder ob jede Handlung eines jeden Kunst ist. Schmuck ist nur tragbar, wenn er den Kunstsinn – und damit die Freiheit – der Trägerin unabhängig von jeder Kunsttheorie achtet (und damit auch die der Männer, die sich über die Halskette und das Gold im Ohrläppchen hinaus zum Schmuck bekennen). Wenn also die Schmuckträgerin durch ihre Wahl einen Akt der Spontaneität, der Selbsttätigkeit setzt, so darf ihr keine Meinung aufgedrängt werden, schon gar nicht durch eine Worterklärung.

Von außen darf eine Kritik – eine Interpretation – versucht werden. Ist der Schmuck des Helfried Kodré wie

[6] Karl Wilhelm Ferdinand Solger, *Vorlesungen über Aesthetik*, Leipzig 1829, S. 102f.

reconciled with ordinary life. An aversion to jewellery leads to overt barbarity."[6]

Schelling, Hegel and Hölderlin write in the work on which they collaborated, known as the "Oldest System Programme": "I am, therefore, convinced that the loftiest act of reason, in encompassing all ideas, is an aesthetic act and that truth and goodness are sisters in beauty alone." If that is true, Helfried Kodré is right: it would be unreasonable to even attempt to give an explanation.

To be sure all this sounds like unattainable ideals; however, a good part of the better life does, after all, consist in seeking enlightenment through ideals.

The theorists of genius and the mechanics of the senses, on the other hand, entirely concur in one thing: what ultimately matters is man's freedom. In so far it makes no difference whether one is an adherent of the theory that everything is art that an artist produces or whether every act of every person is art. Jewellery is only wearable if it respects the feeling for art – and, therefore, the freedom – of the woman wearing it independently of all art theory (and concomitantly also the freedom of the men who admit to a love for jewellery above and beyond the necklace and gold on the ear lobe). If, therefore, the woman wearing jewellery has shown in her choice an act of spontaneity, of independence, no one may impose an opinion on her, certainly not through a verbal declaration.

From outside a critique – an interpretation – may be attempted. Is Helfried Kodré's jewellery like a Mozart piano concerto? The composer wrote to his father on 28 December 1782: "The concertos are in fact the thing in-between too difficult and too easy – are very brilliant – pleasing to the ears – naturally without falling into emptiness – here and there – also connoisseurs alone

[6] Karl Wilhelm Ferdinand Solger, *Vorlesungen über Aesthetik*, Leipzig 1829, p. 102f.

  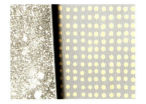

ein Klavierkonzert von Mozart? Der Komponist schrieb am 28. Dezember 1782 an seinen Vater: „Die Concerten sind eben das Mittelding zwischen zu schwer, und zu leicht – sind sehr Brilliant – angenehm in die Ohren – Natürlich, ohne in das leere zu fallen – hie und da – können auch Kenner allein satisfaction erhalten – doch so – dass die Nichtkenner damit zufrieden seyn müssen, ohne zu wissen warum."

Es ist Helfried Kodré sehr wichtig, dass sein Schmuck nicht ausschließlich über das Geistige wirkt. Jedes Erlebnis – natürlich auch das Kunsterlebnis – wird einen Teil haben, der unmittelbar über die Sinne auf das Gemüt eindringt. Der Reiz und der Affekt sind vorhanden und sollen auch gar nicht ausgeschlossen werden, schon gar nicht vom Schmuck.

Viele kommen nicht umhin, den Reflex zu überlegen – die einen mehr, die anderen weniger. Dabei werden Erfahrung, Zuwendung, Bereitschaft und das Wissen des Aufnehmenden sehr beeinflussen, ob es bei einer bloß reizvollen Begegnung bleibt oder ob das Erlebnis zur Erfahrung wird. Das Besondere an Kodrés Schmuck liegt nun darin, dass er zwar zuerst das Gemüt der Trägerin anspricht, es ihr dann aber überlässt, sich mit dem Werk zu inszenieren. Hier setzt also das „Mach' mich schön" der Eva Kodré-Klingenstein an, von Helfried Kodré nicht nur mitgetragen, sondern unterstützt.

Schönheit macht anziehend, Schönheit strebt nach Vereinigung. Schönheit lädt den anderen ein, um eine Verbindung zu werben und die Vielfalt der eigenen Persönlichkeit aufzudecken und somit brauchbar zu machen. Viel ist über den ökonomischen Austausch der Schönheit geschrieben worden. Solger hat Recht, es ist auch gegen den Zierrat als bloßen Putz nichts einzuwenden. Die Lust am Angenehmen ist nicht böse, nicht von vornherein. Es ist nichts Schlechtes, die Aufmerksamkeit zu wecken.

Helfried Kodré ist sich immer bewusst, dass er das ihm Eigene und das Eigene seiner Zeit darzustellen hat. Doch es

can receive satisfaction – yet so – that non-connoisseurs must be satisfied without knowing why."

It is very important to Helfried Kodré that his jewellery should not make the impact it does solely through the intellect. Every experience – naturally the experience of art as well – will have a share in what penetrates to the feelings directly through the senses. Attraction and affect are there and should not be excluded, certainly not from jewellery.

Many cannot avoid thinking about the reflex – some more, some less. In this process experience, devotion, readiness and the knowledge of the recipient will have a strong influence on whether an experience is to remain merely a charming encounter or whether it will be formative. What is so special about Kodré's jewellery lies in the circumstance that he first addresses the wearer's feelings but then leaves it up to her to stage herself with the work. This is the point at which Eva Kodré-Klingenstein's "make me beautiful" takes hold, not only with Helfried Kodré's approval but also with his support.

Beauty makes attractive, beauty strives for union. Beauty invites others to court an alliance and to reveal the many facets of one's own personality and thus make it useful. Much has been written about the beauty as barter. Solger is right; there is nothing to object to in adornment as mere finery. Pleasure in what is pleasant is not evil, not *a priori*. There is nothing bad about attracting attention.

Helfried Kodré has always been aware that he had to represent what is distinctively his own and what is characteristic of his time. However, there is also a commitment to "intrinsic necessity" and then "purposively touching the human soul" with the "element of the pure-and-eternal-artistic, which goes through all people, peoples and times, is to be seen in the art work of every artist of every nation and every era and as the primary element of art knows no space and no time."[7]

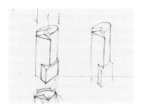  

gibt auch die Verpflichtung gegenüber der „inneren Notwendigkeit" und dann die „zweckmäßige Berührung der menschlichen Seele" mit dem „Element des Rein-und-Ewig-Künstlerischen, welches durch alle Menschen, Völker und Zeiten geht, im Kunstwerk jedes Künstlers jeder Nation und jeder Epoche zu sehen ist und als Hauptelement der Kunst keinen Raum und keine Zeit kennt."[7]

Mit seiner Vorliebe für den Vorhand-Topspin im Tennis hat Helfried Kodré einen Hinweis gegeben. Fallen innere Notwendigkeit und mechanischer Ablauf zusammen, so kann dies zu einem ekstatischen Erlebnis führen. Der Autodidakt Kodré arbeitet in der Metallbearbeitung und -verbindung mit Ingenuität und einem Vollständigkeitsstreben, das über das Selbstverständnis eines präzisen Handwerks weit hinausgeht. Die Verletzung der Kante eines Schmuckstückes bereitet ihm physische Schmerzen. Die Genauigkeit der Form ist das Maß des Unendlichen. Die Vollkommenheit – auch im Unendlichen – ist ohne Maß nicht denkbar. Die Vollkommenheit ist nichts Unbestimmtes, sie zeigt sich im notwendigen und allgemeingültigen Verhältnis der Massen und Maße, in der Lichtwirkung der Oberfläche und im Gewicht. Nur – was ist die Vollkommenheit ohne den Menschen, der sie empfindet?

Helfried Kodré hat auch Schelling gelesen; als rauschhafter Hintergrund werden hier vier Schelling-Stellen wiedergegeben:

„Objekt der Konstruktion und dadurch der Philosophie ist überhaupt nur, was fähig ist, als Besonderes das Unendliche in sich aufzunehmen. Die Kunst, um Objekt der Philosophie zu sein, muss also überhaupt das Unendliche in sich als Besonderem entweder wirklich darstellen oder es wenigstens darstellen können. Da die Kunst der Philosophie so genau entspricht, und selbst nur ihr vollkommenster objektiver Reflex ist, so muss sie auch durchaus alle Potenzen durchlaufen, welche die Philosophie im Idealen durchläuft,

[7] Wassily Kandinsky, *Über das Geistige in der Kunst*, München 1912, S. 47–56, 78f., 87, 93.

With his preference for forehand top spin in tennis, Helfried Kodré has given a clue. If intrinsic necessity and mechanical sequence coincide, this can lead to an ecstatic experience. Entirely self-taught, Kodré works at processing metal and linking it with ingenuity and a striving for perfection which goes far beyond any notions of precise workmanship. Injuring the edge of a piece of jewellery causes him physical pain. Precision of form is the measure of the infinite. Perfection – even in the infinite – is unthinkable without measure. Perfection is nothing indeterminate; it is revealed in the necessary and universally valid relationship of masses and proportions, in the effect of light on a surface and in weight. Only – what is perfection without a person to feel it?

Helfried Kodré has also read Schelling; as background sounds of an intellectual orgy not to be grasped by reason or intellect, four Schelling passages are cited here:

"The object of construction and, therefore, of philosophy is indeed only what is capable of subsuming the infinite in itself as exceptional. Art, in order to be the object of philosophy, must, therefore, indeed either really represent the infinite in itself as exceptional or at least be able to represent it. Since art so precisely matches philosophy and itself is only its most perfect objective reflection, it must also definitely go through all powers which philosophy goes through in the ideal and this one thing suffices to relieve us of our doubts about the method necessary for our science."

"The fundamental character of the work of art is, therefore, an unconscious infinity (synthesis of nature and freedom). In addition, the artist seems in his work, what he has put into it with evident intention, to have represented an infinity, instinctively, as it were, which no finite mind is capable of entirely developing."

[7] Wassily Kandinsky, *Über das Geistige in der Kunst*, Munich 1912, pp. 47–56, 78f., 87, 93.

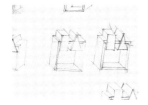

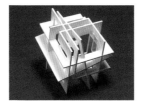

Kleinskulptur/Miniature sculpture, 2001

und dieses Eine reicht hin, um uns über die notwendige Methode unserer Wissenschaft außer Zweifel zu setzen".

„Der Grundcharakter des Kunstwerkes ist also eine bewusstlose Unendlichkeit (Synthese von Natur und Freiheit). Der Künstler scheint in seinem Werk außerdem, was er mit offenbarer Absicht darein gelegt hat, instinctmäßig gleichsam eine Unendlichkeit dargestellt zu haben, welche ganz zu entwickeln kein endlicher Verstand fähig ist."

„Jede ästhetische Production geht aus vom Gefühl eines unendlichen Widerspruchs, also muss auch das Gefühl, was die Vollendung des Kunstproductes begleitet, das Gefühl einer solchen Befriedigung seyn und dieses Gefühl muss auch wieder nur in das Kunstwerk selbst übergehen. Der äußere Ausdruck des Kunstwerks ist also der Ausdruck der Ruhe und der stillen Größe, selbst da, wo die höchste Spannung des Schmerzes oder der Freude ausgedrückt werden soll. Wir werden das Unendliche als das unbedingte Prinzip der Kunst dartun müssen." „Wie für die Philosophie das Absolute das Urbild der Wahrheit – so für die Kunst das Urbild der Schönheit. Wir werden daher zeigen müssen, dass Wahrheit und Schönheit nur zwei verschiedene Betrachtungsweisen des Einen Absoluten sind".

Helfried Kodré ist aber nicht Romantiker, sondern Skeptiker. In das Gleichmaß der Formen ragt der Keil der Unmöglichkeit. Der Kreis ist aufgebrochen; der Radius wird fast zur Schneide. Ein kantiger Stab krümmt sich unterwegs, setzt sich noch kurz fort und endet dann. Ein flaches Dreieck – auch mit Assoziationen zu einem geometrischen Zeichengerät – funktioniert als solches nicht, weil ein Schenkel unversehens nach außen kurvt. Die Blätter des „Goldenen Zweiges" (siehe Abb. 40) ruhen nicht auf einem geraden Stamm, sondern die Ringschiene ist seltsam windschief geworden. – Hat sie der Wind des Zweifels erfasst? Die Würfel haben keine Seitenwände. Sie werden

"Every aesthetic production derives from the feeling of an infinite contradiction; therefore, the feeling which accompanies the completion of an art product must also be the feeling of such satisfaction and this feeling must also lead only to the art work itself. The external expression of the work of art is, therefore, the expression of tranquillity and tacit greatness, even there where the greatest tension of pain or joy is to be expressed. We will have to make the infinite the unconditional principle of art."

"As the absolute is the primal image of truth for philosophy – so for art the primal image of beauty. Consequently, we shall have to demonstrate that truth and beauty are only two different ways of looking at the One Absolute."

Helfried Kodré is, however, not a Romantic; he is a sceptic. The wedge of impossibility sticks into the evenness of forms. The circle is broken into; the radius almost becomes the cutting edge. An angular rod curves underway, continues for a short way and then ends. A flat triangle – also with associations of a geometric drawing implement – does not function as such because a leg of the triangle accidentally curves outwards. The leaves of the "Golden Bough" (see ill. 40) do not rest on a straight trunk but the side of the ring has become oddly skewed by the wind. – Has the wind of doubt touched it? The cubes have no side walls. They are held together by a system of struts which makes construction as such a questionable subject.

Despite all this, charm and beauty are unbroken; what is broken is the certainty of redemption.

The monument character of each work of Kodré's is evident. Perfection is unattainable.

Helfried Kodré makes monuments to the desire for perfection.

In so doing, has he – in the sense of the exhortation by Boethius at the beginning – united the beginning with the

Helfried Kodré, Heidi Bollmann, Renzo Pasquale, Annamaria Zanella, Karl Bollmann

durch ein System von Stützen zusammen gehalten, das die Konstruktion an sich zum fragwürdigen Thema macht.

Bei alledem sind Reiz und Schönheit ungebrochen; gebrochen ist die Sicherheit der Erlösung.

Der Monumentcharakter einer jeden Arbeit Kodrés ist evident. Vollkommenheit ist nicht zu erreichen.

Helfried Kodré macht Denkmäler der Sehnsucht nach dem Vollkommenen.

Hat er damit – im Sinne der Eingangsforderung des Boethius – in der ewigen Ordnung den Anfang mit dem Ende geeint? Wohl nicht. Es ist unmöglich. Aber er macht den idealen Schmuck, die Möglichkeit der Verbindung von Menschen. Nichts eint mehr als die Sehnsucht nach dem Vollkommenen.

end in the eternal order? Probably not. That is impossible. But he makes ideal jewellery, the possibility of connecting people. Nothing unites more than the yearning for perfection.

Skulptur im öffentlichen Raum
„L'ACQUA DURA Progetti di scultura per la riviera del Brenta"
Villa Ferretti Angeli in Dolo (Vincenzo Scamozzi, 1596)
mit Skulpturen-Projekt „Ferroarcangelo", 2000, Corten-Stahl, H 3,5 m

Sculpture in public space
"L'ACQUA DURA Progetti di scultura per la riviera del Brenta"
Villa Ferretti Angeli in Dolo (Vincenzo Scamozzi, 1596) and
sculpture project "Ferroarcangelo", 2000, Corten steel, h. 3.5 m

Katalog / Catalogue
Arbeiten von Helfried Kodré 1990 – 2006 / **The Work of Helfried Kodré 1990 – 2006**

1
Armband
1990, Gold, Weißgold, Silber, Palladium, 7×5×6,5 cm, Privatsammlung Deutschland

1
Bracelet
1990, gold, white gold, silver, palladium, 7×5×6.5 cm, private collection Germany

2

3 Ringe
1991, 1991, 1993; Weißgold, Silber, Palladium; Silber, Palladium; Gold, Weißgold, Silber, Palladium; 4,3×4 cm, 4×4,3 cm, 3,5×4 cm; Sammlung des Künstlers, Privatsammlung Österreich, Schmuckmuseum Pforzheim (von oben nach unten)

2

3 rings
1991, 1991, 1993; white gold, silver, palladium; silver, palladium; gold, white gold, silver, palladium; 4.3×4 cm, 4×4.3 cm, 3.5×4 cm; collection of the artist, private collection Austria, Schmuckmuseum Pforzheim (top down)

Zeichnung Drawing

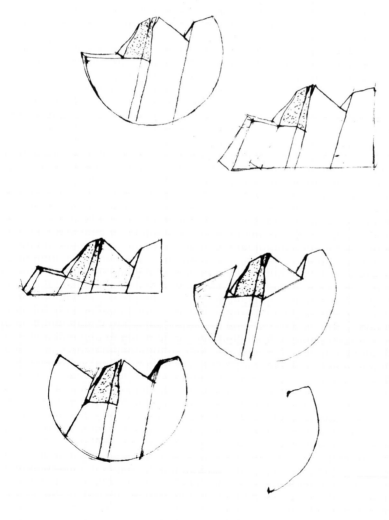

3 **Brosche** 1993, Silber, Gold, Weißgold, 7×5,5 cm, Privatsammlung Deutschland	**3** **Brooch** 1993, silver, gold, white gold, 7×5.5 cm, private collection Germany
4 **Ohrschmuck** 1993, Weißgold, Gold, 5×2 cm, Sammlung des Künstlers	**4** **Ear jewellery** 1993, white gold, gold, 5×2 cm, collection of the artist
5 **Brosche** 1993, Silber, Weißgold, Gold, Palladium, 7×4 cm, Privatsammlung Österreich	**5** **Brooch** 1993, silver, white gold, gold, palladium, 7×4 cm, private collection Austria
6 **Ring** 1994, Weißgold, Gold, Palladium, 2,3×2×1,8 cm, Privatsammlung Österreich	**6** **Ring** 1994, white gold, gold, palladium, 2.3×2×1.8 cm, private collection Austria

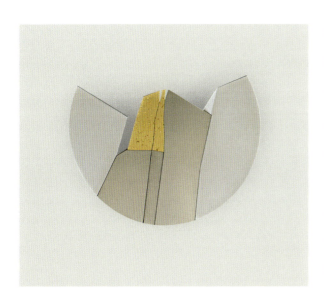

7
2 Ringe
1994; Weißgold, Gold;
3,6×2,5×0,7 cm,
3,5×2,5×0,7 cm; Sammlung
Helga Pessl, Wien,
Privatsammlung Österreich

7
2 rings
1994; white gold, gold;
3.6×2.5×0.7 cm,
3.5×2.5×0.7 cm; Helga Pessl
collection, Vienna,
private collection Austria

8

3 Broschen
1994; Weißgold, Gold;
Weißgold, Gold, Palladium;
Weißgold, Gold; 11,5×1 cm,
10,5×1,5 cm, 10,6×1,3 cm;
Schmuckmuseum Pforzheim,
Privatsammlung Österreich
(2×)

8

3 brooches
1994; white gold, gold; white
gold, gold, palladium; white
gold, gold; 11.5×1 cm,
10.5×1.5 cm, 10.6×1.3 cm;
Schmuckmuseum Pforzheim,
private collection Austria
(2×)

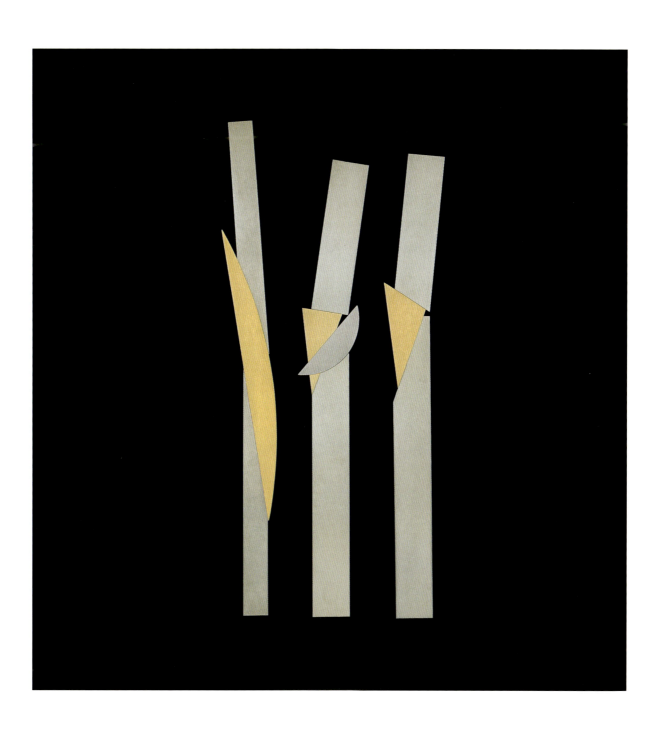

9
Kleinskulptur
1991, Silber, 7,5×3,5 cm,
Sammlung des Künstlers

9
Miniature sculpture
1991, silver, 7.5×3.5 cm,
collection of the artist

10
Kleinskulptur
1992, Silber, H 19 cm,
Sammlung Bernhard
Leitner, Wien

10
Miniature sculpture
1992, silver, h. 19 cm,
Bernhard Leitner
collection, Vienna

11
2 Broschen
1993, Silber, 9×2 cm,
7,5×3×1,5 cm,
Privatsammlung Österreich

11
2 brooches
1993, silver, 9×2 cm,
7.5×3×1.5 cm,
private collection Austria

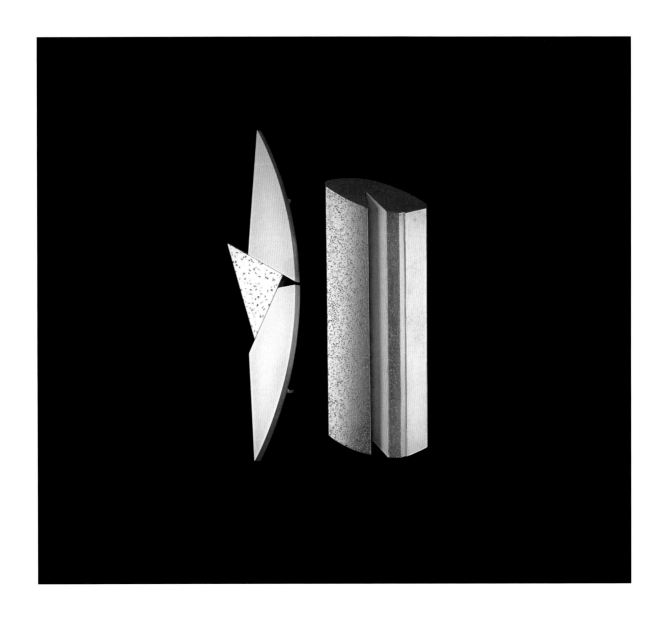

12
Brosche
1993, Silber, 7×4 cm,
Sammlung Walter und
Maria Holzer

12
Brooch
1993, silver, 7×4 cm,
Walter and Maria
Holzer collection

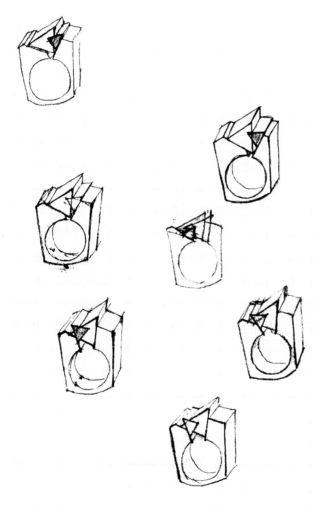

13	**13**
Ring	Ring
1996, Weißgold, Lapislazuli, 3,5×3×1 cm, Artothek des Bundes, Österreich, Dauerleihgabe im Museum für angewandte Kunst (MAK), Wien	1996, white gold, lapis lazuli, 3.5×3×1 cm, Artothek des Bundes, Austria, on permanent loan to the Museum of angewandte Kunst (MAK), Vienna
15	**15**
Ring	Ring
1996, Silber, Lapislazuli, 3,5×3,5×1,2 cm, Privatsammlung Österreich	1996, silver, lapis lazuli, 3.5×3.5×1.2 cm, private collection Austria
14	**14**
Ring	Ring
1996, Weißgold, Gold, Palladium, 3×2,5×1,2 cm, Privatsammlung Italien	1996, white gold, gold, palladium, 3×2.5×1.2 cm, private collection Italy
16	**16**
2 Ringe	2 rings
1994, Weißgold, Gold, 3,2×2,5×0,7 cm, Sammlung des Künstlers, Privatsammlung Österreich	1994, white gold, gold, 3.2×2.5×0.7 cm, collection of the artist, private collection Austria

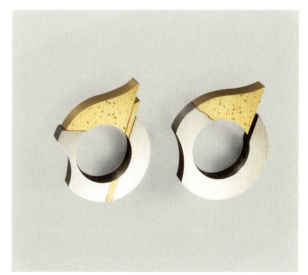

17	17
Ohrschmuck	**Ear jewellery**
1996, Gold, 5×3×0,8 cm,	1996, gold, 5×3×0.8 cm,
Privatsammlung Schweiz	private collection Switzerland

18
Ohrschmuck
1995, Gold, 2,5×2,7×0,8 cm,
Privatsammlung Österreich

18
Ear jewellery
1995, gold, 2.5×2.7×0.8 cm,
private collection Austria

19

2 Broschen
1997; Gold, Silber; 11,5×2 cm,
12,5×2,5 cm;
Sammlung des Künstlers,
Sammlung Bollmann

19

2 brooches
1997; gold, silver; 11.5×2 cm,
12.5×2.5 cm;
collection of the artist,
Bollmann collection

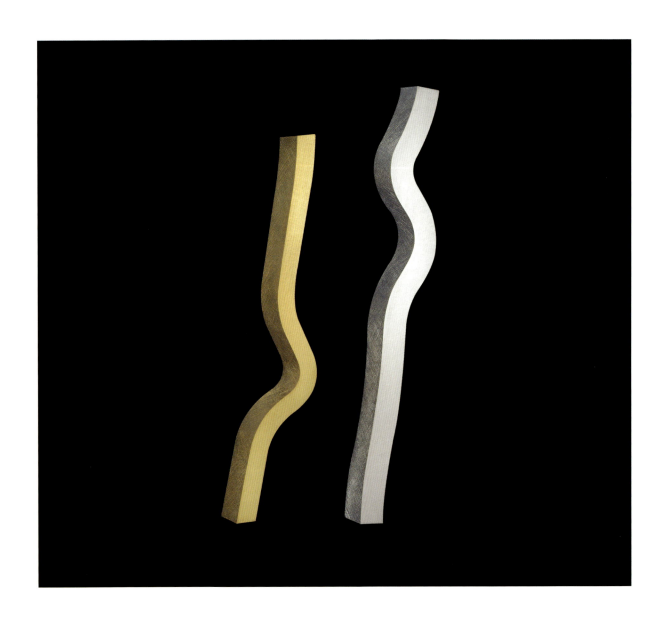

20 2 Broschen 1997, Gold, 11×1,5 cm, Privatsammlung Österreich, Sammlung des Künstlers	**20** 2 brooches 1997, gold, 11×1.5 cm, private collection Austria, collection of the artist

21 2 Broschen 1997, Silber, 13×2,5 cm, 13×2 cm, Privatsammlung Deutschland, Privatsammlung Österreich	**21** 2 brooches 1997, silver, 13×2.5 cm, 13×2 cm, private collection Germany, private collection Austria

22
Brosche
1997, Silber, Gold,
11,5×1,5 cm,
Privatsammlung Österreich

22
Brooch
1997, silver, gold,
11.5×1.5 cm,
private collection Austria

23
2 Broschen
1997, Gold, Silber, 11,3×2 cm,
11,7×1,5 cm,
Sammlung des Künstlers

23
2 brooches
1997, gold, silver, 11.3×2 cm,
11.7×1.5 cm,
collection of the artist

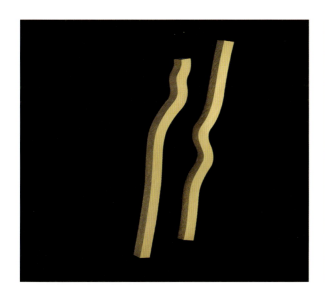
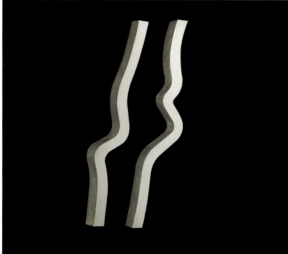
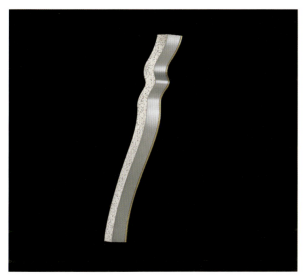
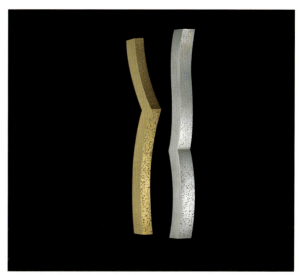

24

3 Broschen
1993, 1997, 2000;
Silber; 9,7×3,2 cm,
13×2,5 cm, 13,5 cm;
Sammlung des Künstlers,
Privatsammlung Deutschland,
Privatsammlung Österreich

24

3 brooches
1993, 1997, 2000;
silver; 9.7×3.2 cm,
13×2.5 cm, 13.5 cm;
collection of the artist,
private collection Germany,
private collection Austria

25
2 Broschen
1997, Silber, 11,5×1,5 cm,
12×3 cm,
Privatsammlung Österreich,
Sammlung des Künstlers

25
2 brooches
1997, silver, 11.5×1.5 cm,
12×3 cm,
private collection Austria,
collection of the artist

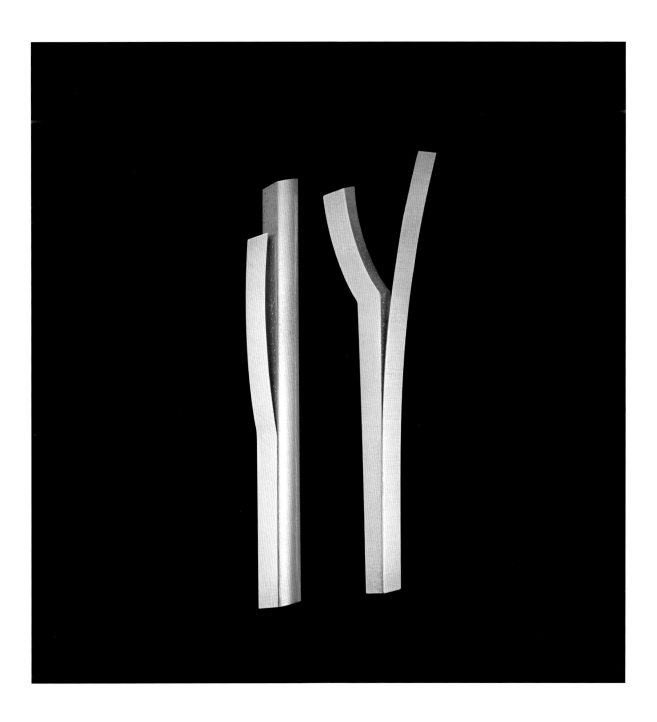

26
Brosche
1996, Silber, 10,5×2,5×1 cm,
Privatsammlung Österreich

26
Brooch
1996, silver, 10.5×2.5×1 cm,
private collection Austria

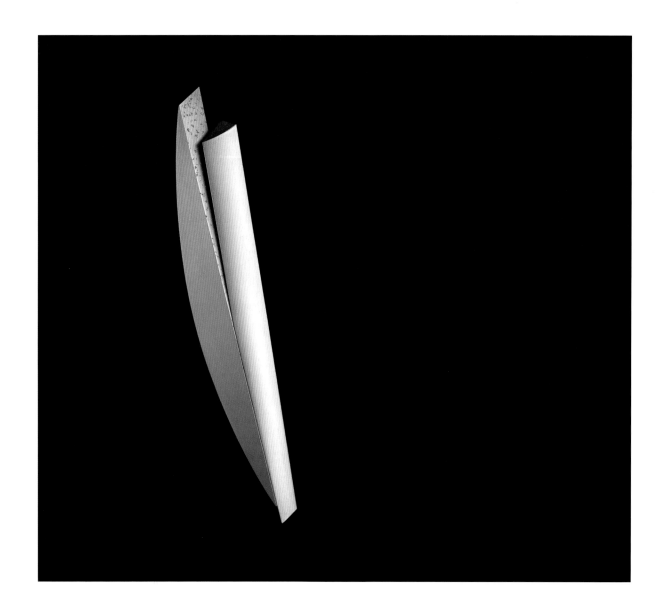

27
Ohrschmuck
1996, Silber, 6×3,3×0,7 cm,
Privatsammlung Österreich

27
Ear jewellery
1996, silver, 6×3.3×0.7 cm,
private collection Austria

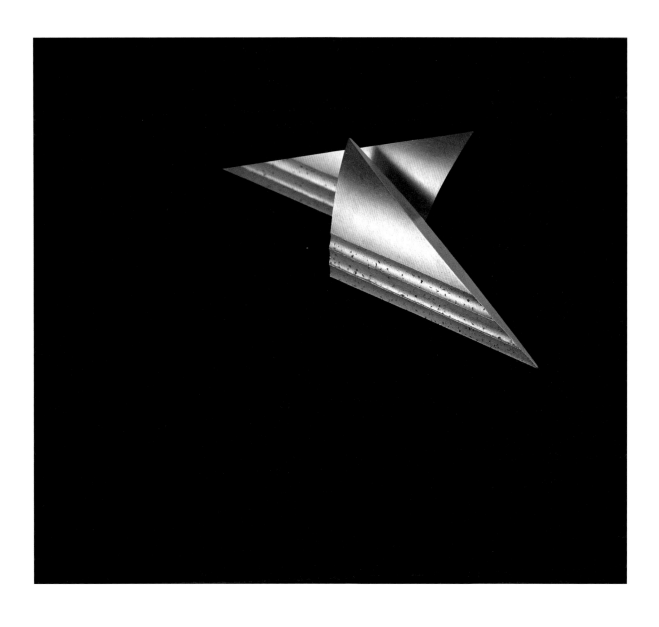

28 **Ohrschmuck** 1998, Silber, 4×2,8 cm, Privatsammlung Österreich	**28** **Ear jewellery** 1998, silver, 4×2.8 cm, private collection Austria
29 **Ohrschmuck** 1998, Silber, 3,5×2,3×1,2 cm, Privatsammlung Schweiz	**29** **Ear jewellery** 1998, silver, 3.5×2.3×1.2 cm, private collection Switzerland
30 **Ohrschmuck** 1997, Gold, 3,5×3 cm, Privatsammlung Österreich	**30** **Ear jewellery** 1997, gold, 3.5×3 cm, private collection Austria
31 **Ohrschmuck** 1997, Silber, 3,5×2,5 cm, Privatsammlung Österreich	**31** **Ear jewellery** 1997, silver, 3.5×2.5 cm, private collection Austria

32
Kleinskulptur
2004, Silber, H 15 cm,
Sammlung des Künstlers

32
Miniature sculpture
2004, silver, h. 15 cm,
collection of the artist

33
Brosche
2000, Silber, 11,5×1,6 cm,
Privatsammlung Italien

33
Brooch
2000, silver, 11.5×1.6 cm,
private collection Italy

34
Brosche
2000, Silber, 8×3,2×2 cm,
Sammlung des Künstlers

34
Brooch
2000, silver, 8×3.2×2 cm,
collection of the artist

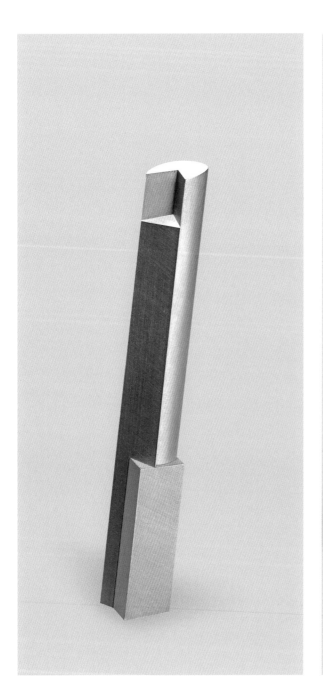

35
Brosche
2000, Silber, 11×2,4×1,4 cm,
Sammlung des Künstlers

35
Brooch
2000, silver, 11×2.4×1.4 cm,
collection of the artist

36 **Ring** 1998, Silber, 3×2,7×1,4 cm, Sammlung des Künstlers	**36** **Ring** 1998, silver, 3×2.7×1.4 cm, collection of the artist
38 **Ring** 1998, Weißgold, Gold, 3,2×3×1,4 cm, Privatsammlung Österreich	**38** **Ring** 1998, white gold, gold, 3.2×3×1.4 cm, private collection Austria

37 **Ring „Amy"** 1999, Weißgold, Gold, 4×3,2×1,5 cm, Privatsammlung USA	**37** **Ring "Amy"** 1999, white gold, gold, 4×3.2×1.5 cm, private collection USA
39 **Ring „Palladio"** 1998, Weißgold, Gold, 3×2,5×1,5 cm, Privatsammlung Italien	**39** **Ring "Palladio"** 1998, white gold, gold, 3×2.5×1.5 cm, private collection Italy

40
Ring „Der Goldene Zweig"
1998, Gold, 3,6×1,4×3,4 cm,
Sammlung Bollmann

40
Ring "The Golden Bough"
1998, gold, 3.6×1.4×3.4 cm,
Bollmann collection

41
Ring „Sambruson"
2000, Weißgold, Gold, Citrin,
2,5×2,4×3cm,
Sammlung des Künstlers

41
Ring "Sambruson"
2000, white gold, gold,
citrine, 2.5×2.4×3cm,
collection of the artist

42
Ring „Sambruson"
s. Abb. 41

42
Ring "Sambruson"
see ill. 41

43
Ring
2006, Silber, Achat,
4,5×3,5×2,2 cm,
Sammlung des Künstlers

43
Ring
2006, silver, agate,
4.5×3.5×2.2 cm,
collection of the artist

44
Ring
2006, Silber, Amazonit,
Farbe, 5×4×2,2 cm,
Sammlung des Künstlers

44
Ring
2006, silver, amazonite,
paint, 5×4×2.2 cm,
collection of the artist

45
Ring
2006, Silber, Türkis,
6,7×3,5×2,2 cm,
Sammlung des Künstlers

45
Ring
2006, silver, turquoise,
6.7×3.5×2.2 cm,
collection of the artist

46
Ring
2006, Silber, Rhodonit,
6×3,5×2,3 cm,
Sammlung des Künstlers

46
Ring
2006, silver, rhodonite,
6×3.5×2.3 cm,
collection of the artist

47
Ring
2006, Silber, Chrysokoll,
7,5×3×2,2 cm,
Sammlung des Künstlers

47
Ring
2006, silver, chrysocolla,
7.5×3×2.2 cm,
collection of the artist

48
Skulptur „Raumtor"
2002, Bronze, 35×53×32 cm,
Sammlung Kulturamt der
Stadt Wien

48
Sculpture "Raumtor"
2002, Bronze, 35×53×32 cm,
collection of the cultural
office of Vienna

49
Skulptur „Raumtor"
s. Abb. 48

49
Sculpture "Raumtor"
see ill. 48

50

Skulptur
2004, Holz, Acrylfarbe,
54×54×59 cm,
Sammlung des Künstlers

50

Sculpture
2004, wood, acrylic,
54×54×59 cm,
collection of the artist

51
Skulptur
2005, Holz, Acrylfarben,
35×34×31 cm,
Sammlung des Künstlers

51
Sculpture
2005, wood, acrylic,
35×34×31 cm,
collection of the artist

52
Skulptur „Große Fuge"
2003, Holz, Acrylfarben,
42×42×42 cm,
Sammlung des Künstlers

52
Sculpture "Große Fuge"
2003, wood, acrylic,
42×42×42 cm,
collection of the artist

53
Skulptur „Große Fuge"
s. Abb. 52

53
Sculpture "Große Fuge"
see ill. 52

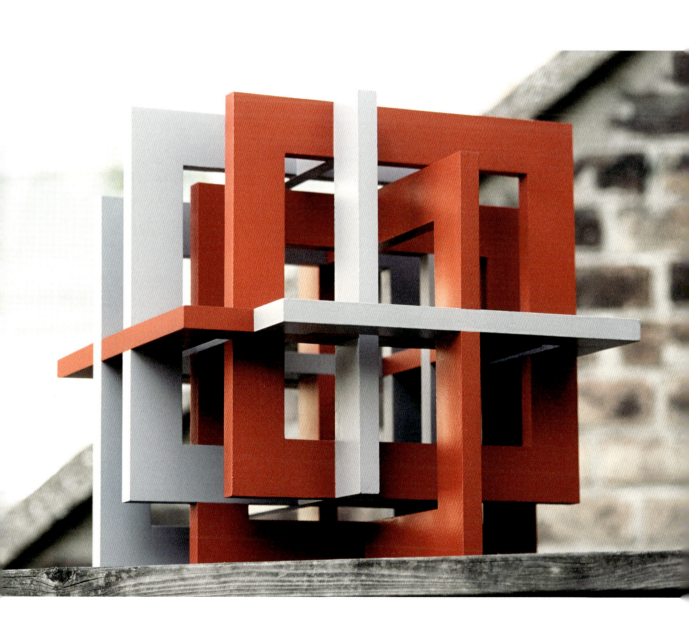

54
Skulptur
2006, Messing, 20×12×12 cm,
Sammlung des Künstlers

54
Sculpture
2006, brass, 20×12×12 cm,
collection of the artist

55
Skulptur
s. Abb. 54

55
Sculpture
see ill. 54

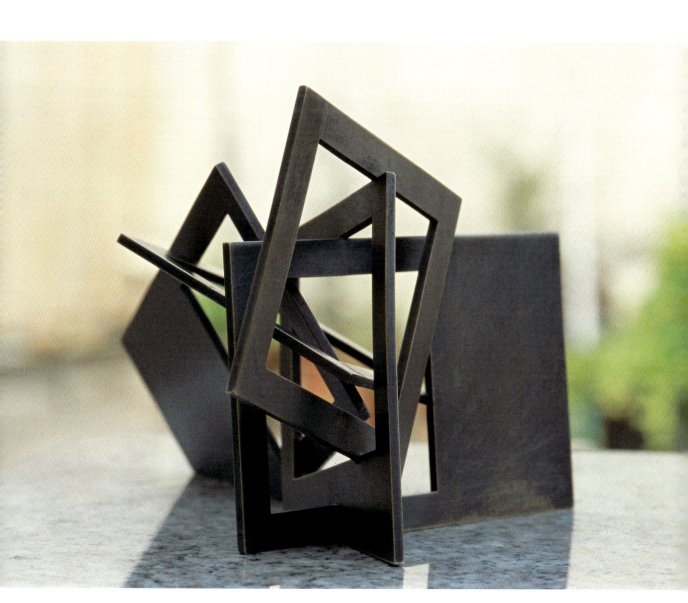

56
Brosche „Eva"
2001, Edelstahl, Silber,
Kupfer, 7×7 cm,
Privatsammlung Österreich

56
Brooch "Eva"
2001, stainless steel, silver,
copper, 7×7 cm, private
collection Austria

57 **Brosche** 2001, Edelstahl, Silber, 8,5×6,5 cm, Sammlung des Künstlers	**57** **Brooch** 2001, stainless steel, silver, 8.5×6.5 cm, collection of the artist
58 **Brosche** 2001, Edelstahl, Silber, 7,5×7 cm, Sammlung des Künstlers	**58** **Brooch** 2001, stainless steel, silver, 7.5×7 cm, collection of the artist
59 **Brosche** 2003, Silber, Gold, Edelstahl, 7,5×7 cm, Sammlung des Künstlers	**59** **Brooch** 2003, silver, gold, stainless steel, 7.5×7 cm, collection of the artist
60 **Brosche** 2002, Gold, Silber, Edelstahl, Kupfer, 7×7 cm, Sammlung Bollmann	**60** **Brooch** 2002, gold, silver, stainless steel, copper, 7×7 cm, Bollmann collection

74 Zeichnung   Drawing

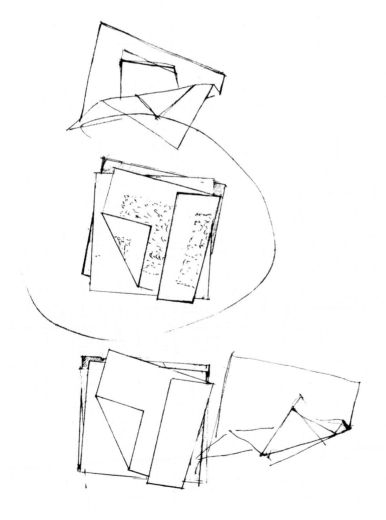

61
Brosche
2002, Gold, Silber,
Edelstahl, 7,5×7,5 cm,
Die Neue Sammlung,
Staatliches Museum für
angewandte Kunst,
Design in der Pinakothek
der Moderne, München

61
Brooch
2002, gold, silver,
stainless steel, 7.5×7.5 cm,
Die Neue Sammlung,
Staatliches Museum für
angewandte Kunst,
Design in der Pinakothek
der Moderne, Munich

62 Brosche „Urbino" 2003, Gold, Silber, Edelstahl, 7×6,5 cm, Sammlung des Künstlers	**62** Brooch "Urbino" 2003, gold, silver, stainless steel, 7×6.5 cm, collection of the artist
64 Brosche „Sabbioneta" 2003, Silber, Gold, 6,7×6,7 cm, Sammlung des Künstlers	**64** Brooch "Sabbioneta" 2003, silver, gold, 6.7×6.7 cm, collection of the artist
63 Brosche 2003, Gold, Silber, Edelstahl, 7×7 cm, Sammlung des Künstlers	**63** Brooch 2003, gold, silver, stainless steel, 7×7 cm, collection of the artist
65 Brosche „Chioggia" 2003, Silber, Gold, 7×7,5 cm, Privatsammlung Österreich	**65** Brooch "Chioggia" 2003, silver, gold, 7×7.5 cm, private collection Austria

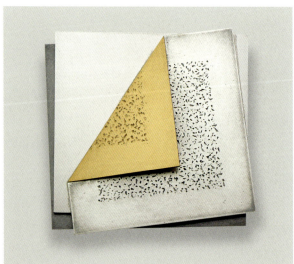

66
Brosche „Panarea"
2006, Silber, Gold,
Lapislazuli, 8×6 cm,
Sammlung des Künstlers

66
Brooch "Panarea"
2006, silver, gold,
lapis lazuli, 8×6 cm,
collection of the artist

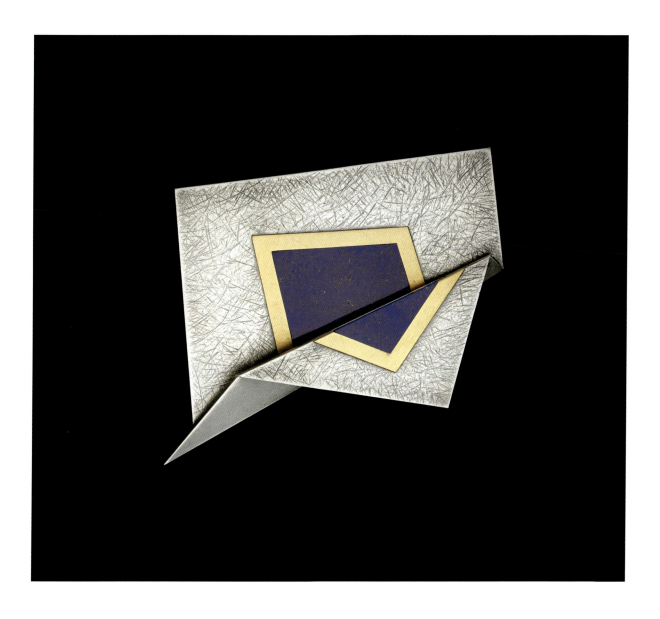

67
Brosche
2003, Silber, Bronze,
12,5×3 cm,
Sammlung des Künstlers

67
Brooch
2003, silver, bronze,
12.5×3 cm,
collection of the artist

68 **Ohrschmuck** 2003, Silber, 5×3,5 cm, Privatsammlung USA	**68** **Ear jewellery** 2003, silver, 5×3.5 cm, private collection USA	**69** **Ohrschmuck** 2002, Silber, 4,5×3,2 cm, Sammlung des Künstlers	**69** **Ear jewellery** 2002, silver, 4.5×3.2 cm, collection of the artist
70 **Ring** s. Abb. 47	**70** **Ring** see ill. 47	**71** **Ohrschmuck** 2005, Silber, Gold, 3,5×2,5 cm, Sammlung des Künstlers	**71** **Ear jewellery** 2005, silver, gold, 3.5×2.5 cm, collection of the artist

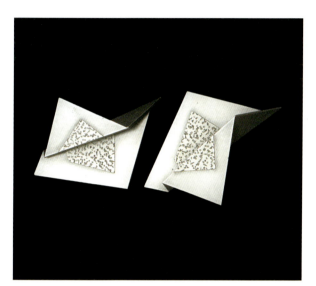

80 Zeichnung   Drawing

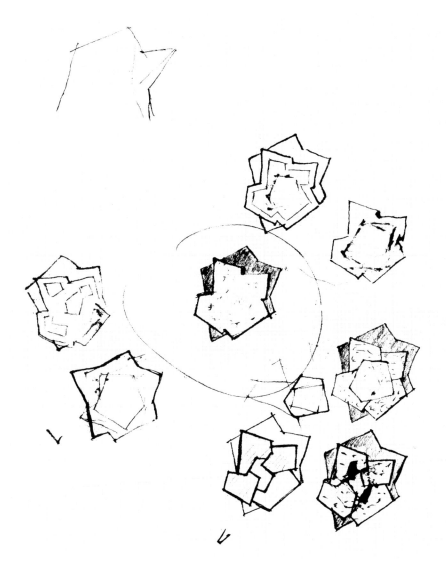

72 **Ohrschmuck** 2002, Silber, 4,5×3,2 cm, Sammlung des Künstlers	**72** **Ear jewellery** 2002, silver, 4.5×3.2 cm, collection of the artist
73 **Ohrschmuck** 2002, Silber, 3,5×4 cm, Sammlung Bollmann	**73** **Ear jewellery** 2002, silver, 3.5×4 cm, Bollmann collection
74 **Ohrschmuck** 2002, Gold, Weißgold, Silber, 4×3,5 cm, Privatsammlung Österreich	**74** **Ear jewellery** 2002, gold, white gold, silver, 4×3.5 cm, private collection Austria
75 **Ohrschmuck** 2002, Silber, 3,5×4 cm, Privatsammlung Österreich	**75** **Ear jewellery** 2002, silver, 3.5×4 cm, private collection Austria

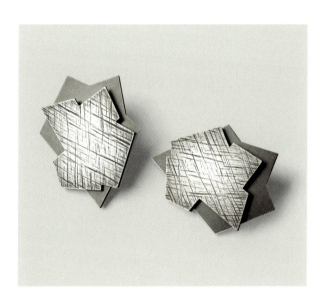

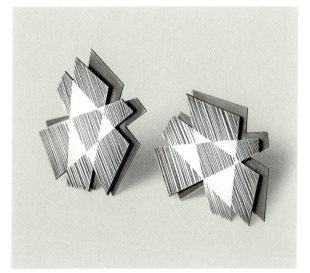

76
Brosche
2004, Silber, 6,5×6,5×2,5 cm,
Sammlung Bollmann

76
Brooch
2004, silver, 6.5×6.5×2.5 cm,
Bollmann collection

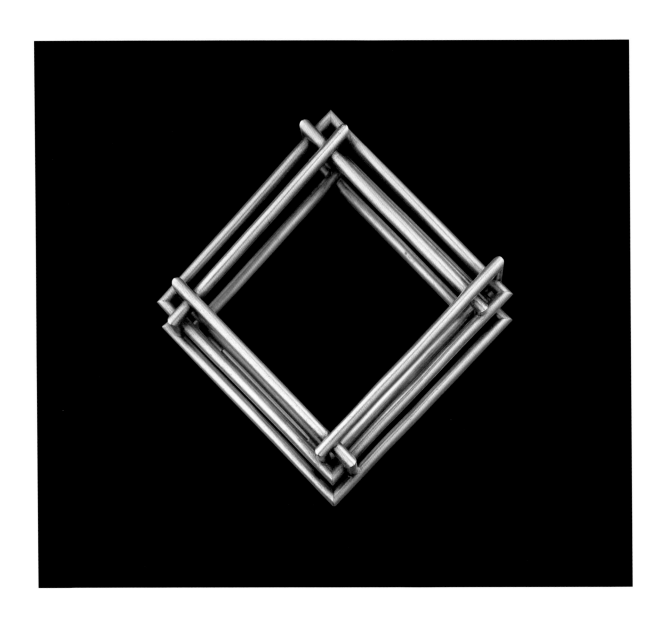

77	**77**
Brosche	Brooch
2004, Silber, 6×6×2 cm,	2004, silver, 6×6×2 cm,
Sammlung des Künstlers	collection of the artist

78	**78**
Brosche	Brooch
2005, Silber, 8×8×2,5 cm,	2005, silver, 8×8×2.5 cm,
Privatsammlung Österreich	private collection Austria

79	**79**
Brosche	Brooch
2004, Silber, 8×6,5 cm,	2004, silver, 8×6.5 cm,
Sammlung Le Arti Orafe Art	collection of Le Arti Orafe Art
Gallery, Florenz	Gallery, Florence

80	**80**
Brosche	Brooch
2005, Silber, 8×7×2,5 cm,	2005, silver, 8×7×2.5 cm,
Privatsammlung Italien	private collection Italy

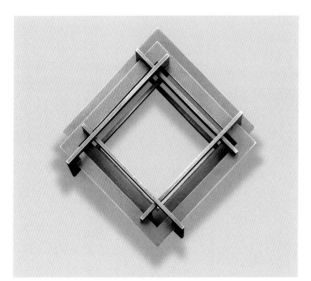

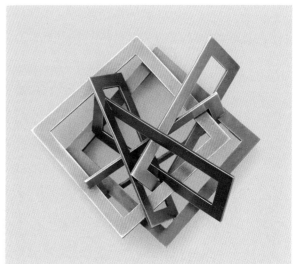

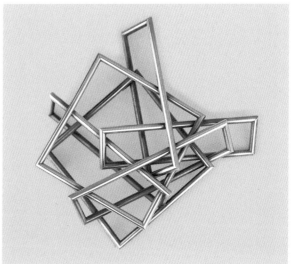

81
Brosche
2006, Silber, Amazonit,
12×11,5 cm,
Sammlung des Künstlers

81
Brooch
2006, silver, amazonite,
12×11.5 cm,
collection of the artist

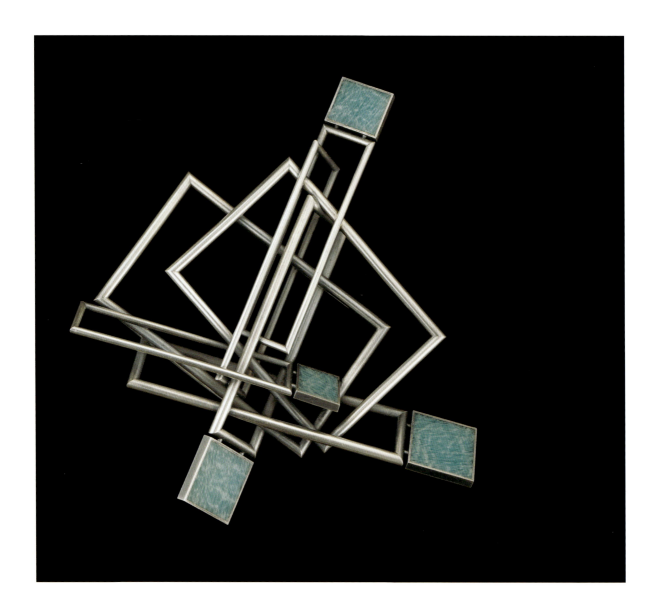

82

Brosche
2005, Silber, Türkis,
12×9,5 cm,
Sammlung Maurer Zilioli,
Desenzano del Garda

82

Brooch
2005, silver, turquoise,
12×9.5 cm,
Maurer Zilioli collection,
Desenzano del Garda

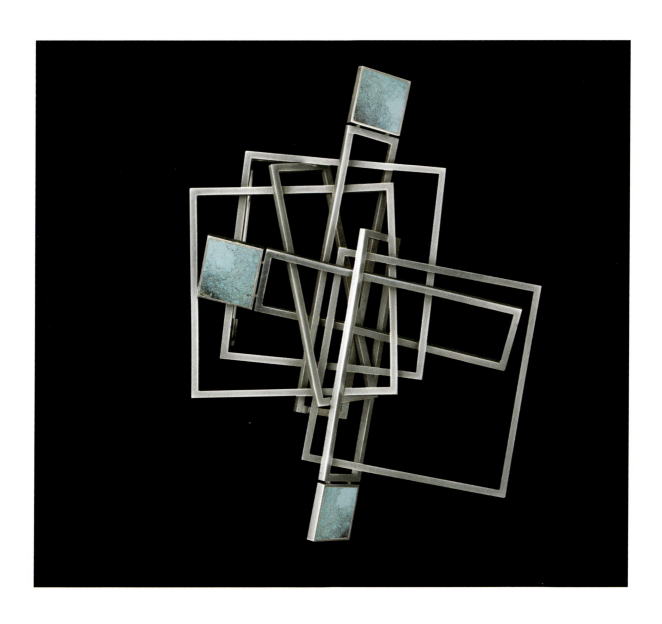

83 **Brosche** 2005, Silber, Türkis-Kunstharz, 9×8cm, Sammlung des Künstlers	**83** **Brooch** 2005, silver, turquoise-synthetic resin, 9×8cm, collection of the artist
84 **Brosche** 2005, Silber, Türkis-Kunstharz, 8,5×8,5cm, Sammung des Künstlers	**84** **Brooch** 2005, silver, turquoise-synthetic resin, 8.5×8.5cm, collection of the artist
85 **Brosche** 2005, Silber, Glas, 10,5×8cm, Privatsammlung Deutschland	**85** **Brooch** 2005, silver, glass, 10.5×8cm, private collection Germany
86 **Ring** 2005, Silber, Rubin-Zoisit, 7,2×3,6×5,7cm, Sammlung Bollmann	**86** **Ring** 2005, silver, ruby-zoisite, 7.2×3.6×5.7cm, Bollmann collection

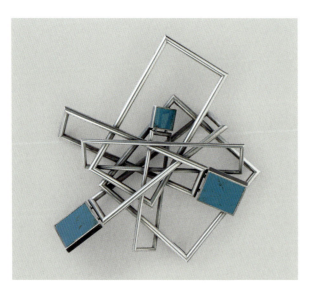

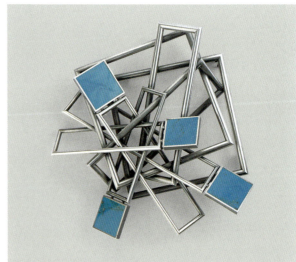

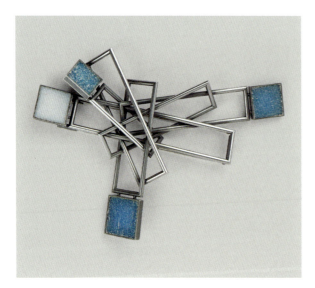

87
Brosche
2005, Silber, Sodalith,
10,5×7 cm,
Sammlung des Künstlers

87
Brooch
2005, silver, sodalite,
10.5×7 cm,
collection of the artist

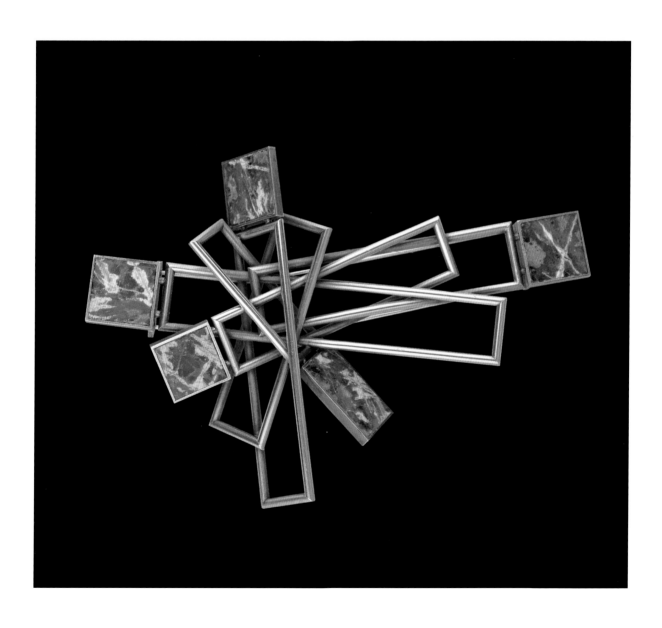

88
Kleinskulptur
„Square Spin"
2005, Silber, 11×11×11 cm,
Sammlung des Künstlers

88
Miniature sculpture
"Square Spin"
2005, silver, 11×11×11 cm,
collection of the artist

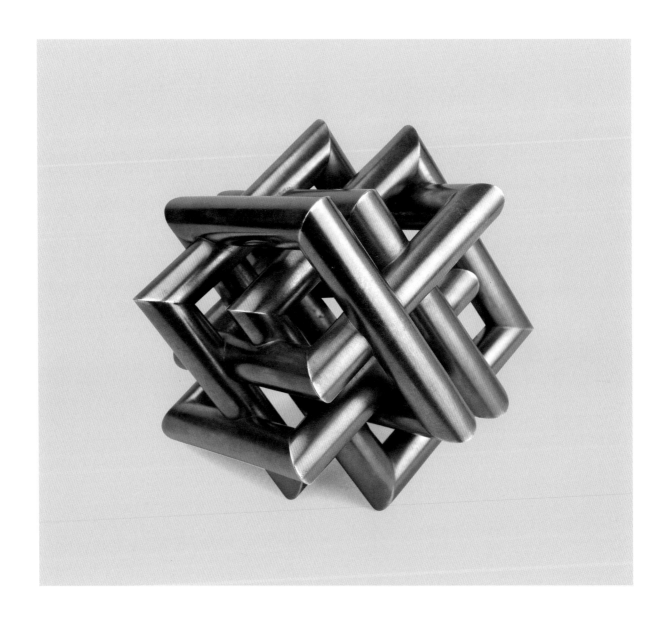

89
Kleinskulptur
2004, Messing, 12×11×10 cm,
Sammlung des Künstlers

89
Miniature sculpture
2004, brass, 12×11×10 cm,
collection of the artist

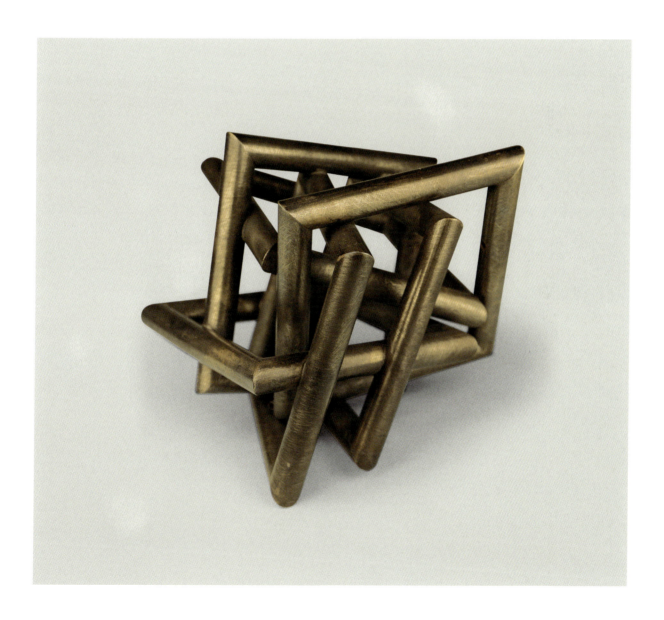

Anhang
Biografie, Sammlungen, Ausstellungen, Preise, Bibliografie

Appendix
Biography, Collections, Exhibitions, Awards, Bibliography

Anhang / Appendix
Biografie / Biography

1940 geboren in Graz (Österreich) **1961–65** Studium der Kunstgeschichte an der Universität Wien **1961** erster Kontakt mit Goldschmiedekunst durch Elisabeth Defner **1962–75** arbeitet als Goldschmied in Werkstattgemeinschaft mit Elisabeth Defner **1964** erste eigenständige Arbeiten und Beginn der Ausstellungstätigkeit **1975–83** nach Unterbrechung seiner Tätigkeit als Schmuckschaffender Fortsetzung und Beendigung des Studiums der Kunstgeschichte **1984** Promotion zum Dr. phil. **1985–96** Lehrbeauftragter am Institut für Kunstgeschichte der Universität Wien **seit 1990** wieder künstlerisch tätig (Schmuck und Skulpturen), zunächst parallel zu seiner Lehrtätigkeit an der Universität Wien **1996** gibt den Lehrauftrag an der Universität Wien auf und konzentriert sich seitdem ausschließlich auf sein künstlerisches Schaffen.

1940 born in Graz, Austria **1961–65** studied art history at Vienna University **1961** first contact with goldsmithing through Elisabeth Defner **1962–75** collaborated with Elisabeth Defner in a joint workshop **1964** first independent work and onset of participating in exhibitions **1975–83** interrupted his work as a jewellery-maker to finish studying art history **1984** took Dr. phil. (PhD) degree **1985–96** instructor at the Art History Institute, Vienna University **since 1990** again working as an artist (jewellery and sculpture), at first in parallel with teaching at Vienna University **1996** ceased teaching at Vienna University to concentrate entirely on his art

Werke in öffentlichen Sammlungen / Works in Public Collections
Einzelausstellungen / Solo Exhibitions

Österreichisches Museum für angewandte Kunst, Wien / Schmuckmuseum Pforzheim / Kunstgewerbemuseum Jablonec / Landesmuseum Joanneum, Graz / Museum für angewandte Kunst, Köln / Artothek Wien / Die Neue Sammlung, Staatliches Museum für angewandte Kunst, Dauerleihgabe der Danner-Stiftung, München / Sammlung der Kulturabteilung der Stadt Wien / Muzeum Ceského Ráje, Turnov

1964 Österreichisches Museum für angewandte Kunst, Wien / Landesmuseum Joanneum, Graz **1967** Kunsthaus am Museum, Köln **1969** Galerie Welz, Salzburg / Galerie Ina Broerse, Amsterdam **1970** Galerie Orfèvre, Düsseldorf **1971** Zentralsparkasse, Wien / Österreichisches Kulturinstitut, Warschau / Galerie Fath, Göppingen **1972** Galerie Arkade Schullin, Graz / Galerie Cardillac, München **1974** Galerie am Graben, Wien / Galerie Alberstraße, Graz **1993** Galerie Slavik, Wien **1995** Electrum Gallery, London **1997** Galerie Slavik, Wien **2000** Galerie iBO, Klagenfurt **2005** „Trasformazioni – Gioielli e sculture", Le Arti Orafe Art Gallery, Florenz

Helfried Kodré

Helfried Kodré, Peter Skubic

Ausstellungs-Beteiligungen / Group Exhibitions

1964 Triennale, Mailand **1966** „Internationales Kunsthandwerk", Stuttgart **1967** „Tendenzen '67", Schmuckmuseum Pforzheim / „Form und Qualität", Handwerksmesse München / „600 Jahre Wiener Goldschmiedekunst", Österreichisches Museum für angewandte Kunst, Wien **1968** Galerii na Betlemsken, Prag / Erstes Internationales Symposium für Silberschmuck, Jablonec **1969** „Form und Qualität", Handwerksmesse München **1970** „International Jewellery Arts Exhibition", Tokio / II. Biennale Internazionale del Gioiello d'Arte, Carrara / „Form und Qualität", Handwerksmesse München / „Tendenzen '70", Schmuckmuseum Pforzheim **1971** „Gold + Silber, Schmuck + Gerät. Von A. Dürer bis zur Gegenwart", Nürnberg / „Form und Qualität", Handwerksmesse München **1972** Galerie „K", Pforzheim / Galerie „At' Home", Toulouse **1973** „Tendenzen '73", Schmuckmuseum Pforzheim / „International Jewellery Arts Exhibition", Tokio / Electrum Gallery, London **1974** „18 Orfèvres d'Aujourd'hui", Lausanne **1976** Galerie Alberstraße, Graz / „International Jewellery Arts Exhibition", Tokio **1979** „Zwei als Eins", Galerie Orfèvre, Düsseldorf **1980** „Schmuck International", Künstlerhaus, Wien / „Schmuck, Zeitgenössische Kunst aus Österreich – Gioiello, Arte Contemporanea d'Austria", Biennale di Venezia, Ateneo San Basso, Venedig **1987** „Bijoux Autrichiens", Europalia, Brüssel **1988** „Schmuck aus Österreich", Galerie Michèle Zeller, Bern **1989** „Ornamenta", Schmuckmuseum Pforzheim / „Schmuck Kunst – Hommage an Sepp Schmölzer", Künstlerhaus Klagenfurt **1990** „Gioielli e Legature – Artisti del XX secolo", Biblioteca Trivulziana, Castello Sforzesco, Mailand (c/o Studio GR 20, Padua) **1994** „Schmuckszene '94", IHM München **1997** „L/M/S – Skulpturen und Objekte", Galerie Menotti, Baden / „SOFA – Sculptures, Objects, Functional Art", Chicago (c/o Galerie Tiller, Wien) / „Zum Lieben – Zeitgenössischer Schmuck", Österreichisches Museum für angewandte Kunst, Wien **1998** „SOFA – Sculptures, Objects, Functional Art", New York (c/o Galerie Tiller, Wien) **1999** „10 Jahre Galerie Slavik", Galerie Slavik, Wien / „Turning Point, Schmuck zur Jahrtausendwende", NÖ Dokumentationszentrum für Moderne Kunst, St. Pölten **2000** „Schmuck 2000", IHM München / „SOFA – Sculptures, Objects, Functional Art", New York (c/o Galerie Tiller Wien) / „The Ego Adorned", Königin Fabiolazaal, Antwerpen / „Turning Point, Schmuck zur Jahrtausendwende", Universität für angewandte Kunst, Wien / „Turning Point, Schmuck zur Jahrtausendwende", Künstlerhaus Klagenfurt / „Alles Schmuck", Museum für Gestaltung, Zürich / „L'ACQUA DURA", Progetti di scultura per la riviera del Brenta, Villa Pisani, Stra **2001** „L'Arte del Gioiello ed il Gioiello d'Artista dal '900 ad oggi", Museo degli Argenti, Florenz / „Mikromegas", Bayerischer Kunstgewerbeverein, München / „Mikromegas", American Crafts Museum, New York / „Radiant Geometries", American Crafts Museum, New York / „Sommer in Salzburg", Galerie iBO im AVA-Hof, Salzburg **2002** „Oreficeria di ricerca", Banque du Gottard, Monte Carlo / „Padova – Vienna. Quattro Stazioni". Gioielleria contemporanea – F. Pavan, A. Zanella, H. Kodré, P. Skubic, Oratorio di San Rocco, Padua / „Mikromegas", Musée de l'Horlogerie et de l'Emaillerie, Genf / „Mikromegas", Hiko Mizuno College of Jewelry, Tokio **2003** „Schmuck '03", IHM München / „Lo Strutturalismo nella Gioielleria Contemporanea", Galleria Entratalibera, Mailand / „Mikromegas", Powerhouse-Museum, Sydney / „Mikromegas", John Curtin Gallery, Curtin University of Technology, Perth / „Mikromegas", Oratorio di San Rocco, Padua / „Re-view. Aspekte Österreichischer Schmuckkunst (1945–2003)", Wako Hall, Tokio **2004** „The Minimal Ring", Confident Gallery, St. Petersburg, Florida / „The Minimal Ring", Bellagio Gallery, Asheville, NC / 16. Schmucksymposium Turnov, Muzeum Ceského Ráje, Turnov **2005** „Joalharia", Museo Nacional de Arqueologia, Lissabon / „8 Jahre – Review-Preview", Galerie iBO, Klagenfurt / „Paradiesfrüchte", Villa Bengel, Idar-Oberstein / „15 Jahre Galerie Slavik", Galerie Slavik, Wien / „Gioielleria Contemporanea, MINIMAL ART", Studio GR 20, Padua **2006** „Gioielleria Contemporanea, MINIMAL ART", Galleria „La Ruota", Cortina d'Ampezzo / „Gioielleria Contemporanea, MINIMAL ART", Galleria Entratalibera, Mailand / „Struttura e Volume", Galleria Maurer Zilioli, Desenzano del Garda / „Attraversamenti". Scultura contemporanea, Galleria Civica, Desenzano del Garda / „Österreichische Schmuckkunst", Galerie Slavik, Wien.

Hubertus von Skal,
Helfried Kodré, 1973

Wolfgang Prohaska

Helfried Kodré,
Ellen Maurer Zilioli

Peter Skubic, Sandra B. Grotta,
Thomas Gentille, Helfried Kodré
in New York, 2001

Anhang / Appendix
Preise / Awards // Bibliografie (Auswahl) / Bibliography (selected)

1967 Bayerischer Staatspreis **1968** Preis des Wiener Kunstfonds **2000** Preis der Stadt Wien für Bildende Kunst

Graham Hughes, *Modern Jewellery*, London 1964 / Gerhard Bott, *Schmuck als künstlerische Aussage unserer Zeit*, Königsbach 1971 / Curt Heigl, *Gold + Silber, Schmuck + Gerät*, Ausst.Kat., Nürnberg 1971 / Fritz Falk (Hrsg.), *Schmuck '73 – Tendenzen*, Ausst.Kat., Pforzheim 1973 / Karl Schollmayer, *Neuer Schmuck – ornamentum humanum*, Tübingen 1974 / Ralph Turner, *Contemporary Jewelry – A Critical Assessment*, London 1976 / K. A. Fleck (Hrsg.), *Jewelry Artists in the World*, Tokio 1976 / Reinhold Reiling, *Goldschmiedekunst*, Pforzheim 1978 / Peter Skubic (Hrsg.), *Schmuck International 1900–1980*, Ausst.Kat., Wien 1980 / Anne Ward, John Cherry, Charlotte Gere, Barbara Cartlidge, *Der Ring im Wandel der Zeit*, München 1981 / Traude Hansen, „Signale der Schmuckkunst", in: *Parnass* 6/84, S. 15–19 / Inge Asenbaum (Hrsg.), *Schmuck, Zeitgenössische Kunst aus Österreich*, Biennale di Venezia, Ausst.Kat., Venedig/Wien 1984 / Barbara Cartlidge, *Twentieth-Century Jewelry*, New York 1985 / P. Vandenbussche (Hrsg.), *Bijoux Autrichiens-Europalia*, Ausst.Kat., Brüssel 1987 / Michèle Zeller (Hrsg.), *Schmuck aus Österreich*, Ausst.Kat., Bern 1988 / Michael Erlhoff, Fritz Falk (Hrsg.), *Ornamenta 1*, Internationale Schmuckkunst, Ausst.Kat., München 1989 / Graziella Folchini Grassetto (Hrsg.), *Gioielli e Legature*, Artisti del XX. Secolo, Ausst.Kat., Mailand 1990 / Verena Formanek, *Wiener Schmuck. Tendenzen 1936–1991*, Wien 1992 / Maria Rennhofer, „Spannung in Silber und Gold – Schmuck von Helfried Kodré", in: *Parnass* 4/93, S. 124–125 / Eva Klingenstein, „Konfrontation und Harmonie. Neue Arbeiten von Helfried Kodré", in: *Weltkunst* 6/94, S. 743–746 / Charlotte Blauensteiner, „Kontrollierte Spannung", in: *Kunsthandwerk & Design* 3/94, S. 40–43 / Peter Nickl (Hrsg.), *Schmuckszene '94*, Ausst.Kat., München 1994 / Maria Rennhofer, „Konzentrierte Form – Komplexe Wirkung. Schmuckobjekte von Helfried Kodré", in: *Parnass* 4/97, S. 130–131 / Eva Klingenstein, „Helfried Kodré: Comeback mit Dynamik", in: *Schmuck Magazin* 5/97, S. 66–69 / Renate Slavik (Hrsg.), *Helfried Kodré*, Wien 1997 / *SOFA – Sculptures, Objects, Functional Art*, Ausst.Kat., Chicago 1997 / *SOFA – Sculptures, Objects, Functional Art*, Ausst.Kat., New York 1998 / M. de Cerval, *Dictionnaire International du Bijou*, Paris 1998 / Fritz Falk, Cornelie Holzach (Hrsg.), *Schmuck der Moderne 1960–1998, Bestandskatalog der modernen Sammlung des Schmuckmuseums Pforzheim*, Stuttgart 1999 / Renate Slavik (Hrsg.), *Schmuck – Kunst am Körper*, Ausst.Kat., Wien 1999 / Susanne Hammer, Fritz Maierhofer (Hrsg.), *turning-point – schmuck aus österreich zur jahrtausendwende*, Ausst.Kat., Wien 1999 / Jan Walgrave (Hrsg.), *Het VerSierde Ego*, Ausst.Kat., Antwerpen 2000 / Reinhold Ludwig, *Hundert Schmuckstücke 2001*, Ulm 2000 / Peter Nickl (Hrsg.), *Schmuck 2000*, Ausst.Kat., München 2000 / *SOFA – Sculpture, Objects, Functional Art*, Ausst.Kat., New York 2000 / M. Mosco, *L'Arte del Gioiello e il Gioiello d'Artista dal '900 ad oggi*, Ausst.Kat., Florenz 2001 / Nancy Preu (Hrsg.), *Radiant Geometries – Fifteen International Jewelers*, Ausst.Kat., New York 2001 / Otto Künzli (Hrsg.), *Mikromegas*, Ausst.Kat., München 2001 / „Sculptures from XS to XL", in: *Arte y Joya* XXVII/148, 2002, S. 138–139 / Kathleen Browne, „Radiant Geometries: Fifteen International Jewelers", in: *Metalsmith*, Bd. 22, Nr. 1, 2002, S. 49 / Roberto Chilleri, „Sul bel Danubio d'Oro – La gioielleria d'autore in Austria", in: *ARTEiN* XV/78, 2002, S. 86–89 / Angela Völker, „Kunsthandwerk und Design", in: Wieland Schmied (Hrsg.), *Geschichte der Bildenden Kunst in Österreich*, Bd. 6: Das 20. Jahrhundert, München 2002 / Graziella Folchini Grassetto, „Helfried Kodré. Un Intellettuale incontra L'Oreficeria", in: *E & F – Eyewear & Fashion*, Nr. 14, 2002,

Annamaria Zanella, Renzo Pasquale, Helfried Kodré

Helfried Kodré, Renzo Pasquale, Francesco Pavan

Hubertus von Skal, Helfried Kodré

S. 12–14 / Graziella Folchini Grassetto, *Padova – Vienna. Quattro Stazioni*, Ausst.Kat., Padua 2002 / Margherita Levorato, Paolo Marcolongo (Hrsg.), „*L'ACQUA DURA", Progetti di Scultura per la Riviera del Brenta*, Sambruson di Dolo 2002 / „La cultura del gioiello tra Padova e Vienna", in: *L'Orafo Italiano* LVI, 2002, S. 117 / „Joyeria contemporánea en Padua", in: *Arte y Joya* XXVIII/152, 2003, S.176–177 / „Joyeria contemporánea en Padua", in: *Eurodesign & Design of the World*, 2003, S. 152–153 / Peter Nickl (Hrsg.), *Schmuck 2003*, Ausst.Kat., München 2003 / Helfried Kodré, „Nouvelle Cuisine – oder zurück an den Anfang. Die Schmuckkunst-Szene der 1970er Jahre", in: *Re-view. Aspekte Österreichischer Schmuckkunst*, Ausst.Kat., Wien 2003 / Antonia Kühnel (Hrsg.), *Re-view. Aspekte Österreichischer Schmuckkunst*, Ausst.Kat., Wien 2003 / Graziella Folchini Grassetto, „Padua – Vienna, Four Stations", in: *Craft Arts* 58, 2003, S. 98–102 / Arch Gregory, *The Minimal Ring*, Waynesville, NC 2004 / Marthe Le Van (Hrsg.), *1000 Rings*, Asheville, NC 2004 / Ellen Maurer Zilioli, „Astrazione e dinamica – Gioielli di Helfried Kodré", in: *Le Arti Orafe Art Gallery* (Hrsg.), *Helfried Kodré – Trasformazioni – Gioielli e Sculture*, Ausst.Kat., Florenz 2005 / Graziella Folchini Grassetto, *Gioielleria Contemporanea MINIMAL ART*, Ausst.Kat., Padua 2005 / Mauro Corradini, „Attraversamenti: ritmi, misure e dismisure nella scultura astratta contemporanea", in: *Attraversamenti, Scultura Contemporanea*, Ausst Kat., Desenzano del Garda 2006.

Künstlerdank / Artist's Acknowledgements

Ich danke vor allem Eva, die mich in den Jahren, in denen die hier gezeigten Arbeiten entstanden sind, immer nach Kräften unterstützt hat. Ohne ihre Hilfe hätte es wohl kaum ausreichend Material zur Veröffentlichung gegeben.
Für das Zustandekommen der Publikation danke ich dem Verlag ARNOLDSCHE Art Publishers und den Sponsoren (BKA Kunst, Wien, Schmuckmuseum Pforzheim und Galerie Slavik, Wien). Ich danke Frank Philippin für die grafische Gestaltung und den Autoren sowie Abigail Prohaska und Rita Siragusa. – Helfried Kodré, September 2006

In particular I thank Eva, who has always supported me with total commitment throughout the years in which the works shown here came into being. Without her help, there would probably not have been enough material to publish.
For making this publication possible, I thank my publishers, ARNOLDSCHE Art Publishers, and my sponsors (BKA Kunst, Vienna, the Schmuckmuseum Pforzheim and Galerie Slavik, Vienna). My thanks go also to Frank Philippin for the graphic design and the authors as well as Abigail Prohaska and Rita Siragusa. – Helfried Kodré, September 2006

GALERIE SLAVIK
www.galerie-slavik.com

Als Galerie für internationale zeitgenössische Schmuckkunst – www.galerie-slavik.com – präsentieren wir künstlerische Vielfalt in höchster Qualität und Einmaligkeit. Als Treffpunkt für Künstler, Sammler, Architekten (architektonisches Juwel) und Kunden aus der ganzen Welt ist es unser Ziel, ein tieferes Verständnis für den faszinierenden Charakter zeitgenössischer Schmuckkunst zu vermitteln.

As a gallery for international contemporary jewellery art – www.galerie-slavik.com – we present a great variety of unique and idiosyncratic works of art of the finest quality. The gallery has become a meeting point for artists, collectors, architects (architectonic jewel) and customers from all over the world and it is our goal to communicate a deeper understanding of the fascinating character of comtemporary jewellery art.

INTERNATIONALE ZEITGENÖSSISCHE SCHMUCKKUNST
A-1010 Wien, Himmelpfortgasse 17
Tel.: +43 1 513 48 12, Fax: +43 1 513 07 48
e-mail: galerie.slavik@vienna.at
Geöffnet: Di-Fr 10-13, 14-18 Uhr, Sa 10-17 Uhr